CASAS TEST PREP STUDENT BOOK

FOR

READING GOALS FORM 903R/904R

LEVEL B

Preparing Adult Learners for CASAS Reading GOALS Tests and for Workforce and College Reading

By Coaching for Better Learning, LLC

CASAS TEST PREP

STUDENT BOOK FOR READING GOALS

FORMS 903R/904R LEVEL B

*Preparing Adult Learners
for CASAS Reading GOALS Tests
&
Workforce and College Reading*

COACHING FOR BETTER LEARNING, LLC

COACHING FOR BETTER LEARNING

TABLE OF CONTENTS

	Introduction	6
Lesson 1	Improving Your Reading	8
Lesson 2	Using Contextual Cues	11
Lesson 3	Types of Text Structures and Linking Words	17
Lesson 4	Using Background Knowledge	24
Lesson 5	Understanding Figurative Language	30
Lesson 6	Understanding Main Ideas and Finding Evidence	39
Lesson 7	Mini-Practice Test	43
Lesson 8	Using K-W-L Charts to Understand Long Passages	46
Lesson 9	Making Inferences and Predictions	53
Lesson 10	Using Imagery	62
Lesson 11	Narrator's Point of View	70
Lesson 12	How to Read Visual Information and Data	76
Lesson 13	More Practice Passages	81
Lesson 14	Final Thoughts	87
Assessment	Reading Practice Test I	88
	Reading Practice Test II	100
	Answer Keys	113
	References	114
	About Coaching for Better Learning	116

INTRODUCTION

This test prep student book is designed to develop adult learners' academic reading skills, preparing them for CASAS Reading GOALS Level B Forms 903R/904R tests and vocational training admission reading tests. In other words, it presents academic reading activities that help adult education programs and workforce programs, along with their learners, meet the Workforce Innovation and Opportunity Act (WIOA) reading expectations.

The reading exercises and answer keys in this student book cover CASAS Reading GOALS Level B standards and College and Career Readiness (CCR) reading standards and content. For example, each lesson focuses on three main areas: ***vocabulary, reading comprehension skills and higher-order reading skills.***

The reading passages presented are from various sources—journal articles, newspaper clippings, and nonfiction and fiction books—covering a wide range of topics. Learners will also be guided to reflect on what they have learned after completing the practice tests at the end of the lessons.

Reading Strategies

This student reading textbook covers and teaches the following reading strategies:

- *Using Background Knowledge*
- *Making Inferences and Predictions*
- *Using Visual Imagery*
- *Identifying Types of Text Structures*
- *Understanding Figurative Language*
- *Building Vocabulary Using Context Clues*
- *Understanding Question-Answer Relationships (QARs)*
- *Learning Nonfiction Text Features*
- *Reading for Main Ideas*
- *Understanding Main Ideas and Finding Evidence*
- *Understanding What You Read*
- *Using Text Structure to Build Reading Comprehension*
- *Understanding Point-of-View*
- *Reading Graphs and Data*

The book is designed for adult learners as an instructional guide for developing reading comprehension skills. It offers academic reading strategies to help learners become more active, strategic and purposeful readers. These strategies will also help learners understand and remember what they read.

Reading is an active thinking process. Therefore, this manual encourages learners to actively engage with texts by predicting, making connections and inferences, asking and answering questions, and completing the comprehension activities.

Additionally, the text provides practice exercises for using the reading strategies to access different texts, e.g., science, social studies, technical and literary. The lessons emphasize text complexity, evidence and knowledge.

Using examples, pictures and text, you will better understand the strategies and how they work. The activities offer hands-on practices, so as you read, study and work through the examples, you will build the confidence to succeed. **You will become a strategic reader**.

Before we start, let's complete the chart below.

WHAT DO I KNOW ABOUT READING SKILLS?	WHY DO I WANT TO IMPROVE MY READING SKILLS?	WHAT AM I MOST EXCITED ABOUT IN IMPROVING MY READING SKILLS?

Now, let's get started!

LESSON 1
IMPROVING YOUR READING

Time and time again, we have heard that the key to improving how we complete an activity is first understanding how to perform it. By reflecting on our performance, we can identify our strengths and weaknesses. Reading is the same way. In this lesson, we will discuss techniques that can help you improve your reading skills.

1.   How am I reading?

Do you find yourself skimming through text to look for pictures and exciting captions? Most of the time, the parts you think are interesting might not tell the whole story. Your brain may be tricking you that it is interesting because you find it easy to understand. However, taking the time to read the entire text might be more enjoyable than you think.

2.   Where do I read?

Do you like to read by yourself? Do you prefer to read in a quiet place? The location you choose to read is essential. You should always choose a comfortable location that will allow you to concentrate fully. The area may also depend on what you are reading. Unless your superpower is reading, you will not fully understand a complex document in a crowded and chaotic place.

3.   What am I reading?

Are you reading a novel or an official document? These two types of writing require different levels of concentration. If you are too comfortable when reading an official document, you may miss important details since your brain and body are in a state of relaxation. Sit upright and focus when reading complex texts.

4.   How do I feel when I read?

Have you ever been in an exam where you are sure you know the answer to a question, but the information evaporates because you are too nervous? Negative emotions can prevent you from reading well and retaining information. Ensure that you practice getting your mind back on track when you lose concentration. Doing this will help you read and perform well, even under pressure.

5.   Should I write down some notes?

If it helps you, why not? This is especially important for exam situations or if you need to complete a task using the text. If appropriate, mark the paragraphs that you think are important. For leisure reading, taking notes is not necessary. Your purpose and the context for reading should tell you if making notes is appropriate.

6. Do I know what all the words mean?

Sometimes, words can be complicated and frustrating to understand. Even the most straightforward words can seem like another language because of how sentences are written. Look up words that prevent you from understanding your reading. It would help if you also use context clues and surrounding words to guess the meaning of unknown vocabulary words.

7. Where do I get confused?

Can you tell when you start to lose focus and when the text becomes confusing? When reading, use a timer so you can notice when you lose focus and stop. Summarize what you understand from the text, then take a break. If appropriate, walking away from the text or closing your eyes for a few minutes may help.

8. Am I patient with myself?

Rome was not built in a day. Therefore, a dash of patience here and there will help you stay motivated. The key is a healthy reward system for exploring different reading materials. For book lovers, a reward system could be getting to start another book. Avoid seeing reading as hard work. Instead, treat it as a way to read writers' minds, travel the world and increase your knowledge.

9. What do I know about the text?

Often you can relate directly or indirectly to reading texts. Ask yourself, "Have I experienced this before?" Try to connect your previous experience to what you are reading.

10. Am I practicing enough?

We read every day. From recipes to texts from our friends, we could argue all of these are "practice." However, we get into problems when we "read to respond" rather than "read to understand." "Reading to understand" involves actively doing a reading activity with a goal in mind. This practice can apply to fiction and non-fiction texts. For example, your purpose for reading a novel is to discover what happens to your favorite character as the story progresses.

PRACTICE EXERCISE

Complete the statements below.

1. I read best when _____

2. I like to read _____

3. I get frustrated when I _____

4. I am most comfortable reading _____

5. Sometimes, when a word is unfamiliar, I _____

6. But now, I will _____

REFLECTION ON LEARNING

Answer the following reflection questions, and feel free to discuss your responses with your teacher or classmate.

- What reading idea or strategy did you learn from this section?

- What new concepts did you learn?

- What methods did you work on in this section?

- What aspect of this section is still not 100 percent clear for you?

- What do you want your teacher to know?

LESSON 2

USING CONTEXTUAL CUES

Even Stephen King, the famous American writer, does not know all the English language words. We often encounter unfamiliar words when we read. In this lesson, you will learn to figure out the meanings of unfamiliar words using contextual cues. We will break the strategies down into two levels: searching for root words and using surrounding words.

Searching for Root Words

Like the roots of a tree, root words provide the foundation of many English words. Prefixes, suffixes or other words add meaning to root words. We can add a *prefix* at the beginning and a *suffix* at the end of a root word.

Below are examples of words you may know:

PREFIX	ROOT WORD	SUFFIX	FULL WORD
In-	**-describe-**	-able	In**describ**able*
Mis-	**-spell-**	-ing	Mis**spell**ing
	Betray-	-al	**Betray**al
	Infect-	-ion	**Infect**ion
In-	-competent		In**competent**
Bi-	**-annual-**	-ly	Bi**annual**ly
Dis-	**-agree**		Dis**agree**

Note: In some cases, you should alter the root word before adding a prefix or suffix. In the first example, the last vowel sound, *e*, is removed.

Now let's use these words to form sentences:

ROOT WORD	FULL WORD	SENTENCE
-describe-	In**describ**able	Jane and Felix were asked to talk about their love for each other. Felix found it easy, but Jane found it difficult. She said their love was **indescribable**.
-spell-	Mis**spell**ing	Callie was angry at what she saw on the official document. There was a **misspelling** that needed to be fixed immediately.
Betray-	**Betray**al	Larry has high standards. Disloyalty and **betrayal** are unacceptable to him.
Infect-	**Infect**ion	I was rushed to the hospital because I had caught an **infection** from being cut by a rusty knife.
-competent	In**competent**	Nadia thought I was **incompetent** because I had just graduated from college and had no experience. I was determined to prove her wrong.
-annual-	Bi**annual**ly	Charlie celebrates his birthday **biannually.** No one knows why.
-dis	Dis**agree**	Shaun and Lucas disagreed on many things, but they agreed that the manager's behavior was disrespectful.

So, we now know that some unfamiliar words are formed using prefixes and suffixes. But what do they mean in the context of the sentences? Let's look at some of the sentences we have made up.

1. Jane and Felix were asked to talk about their love for each other. Felix found it easy, but Jane found it difficult. She said their love was **indescribable**.

We understand that the root word **describe** means "giving a detailed account of something." Therefore, we can understand that the word **indescribable** is used to explain that Jane cannot provide a lot of details about their love.

2. Callie was angry at what she saw on the official document. There was a crucial **misspelling** that needed to be fixed immediately.

We understand that the root word **spell** means "writing a word using the correct sequence." Therefore, we can understand that the word **misspelling** is used to explain that there was a word in the official document that was not written correctly.

3. Larry has high standards. Disloyalty and **betrayal** are unacceptable to him.

We understand that the root word **betray** means "revealing information about someone else, whether you meant to or not." Therefore, we can understand that the word **betrayal** explains Larry's expectations that the people he talks to will not share his information with others.

4. I was rushed to the hospital because I had caught an **infection** from being cut by a rusty knife.

We understand that the root word **infect** means "to affect or contaminate." Therefore, we can understand that the word **infection** explains that the character's wound was affected/contaminated because the knife was rusty.

5. Tallie thought I was **incompetent** because I had just graduated from college and had no experience. I was determined to prove her wrong.

We understand that the root word **competent** means "being able to perform well and meet adequate standards." Therefore, we can understand that the word **incompetent** is used to explain that Tallie thinks the other character cannot perform and meet adequate standards.

EXERCISE 1

Can you explain the rest of the sentences?

1. Charlie celebrates his birthday **biannually.** No one knows why.

    a. What does the root word mean?

    _____

    b. How has the writer used the word in the sentence?
       The writer has used the word to mean that

    _____

2. Shaun and Lucas **disagreed** on many things, but they agreed that the manager's behavior was disrespectful.

    a. What does the root word mean?

    _____

    b. How has the writer used the word in the sentence?
       The writer has used the word to mean that

    _____

Paying Attention to Surrounding Words

12

Another good technique for finding the meaning of an unfamiliar word is to look at other words that come before and after it. Ask yourself, "Is there a similar word that can be used to replace it?"

Let us have a look at a few sentences:

a. Movie star Brad Pitt's home was large, beautiful and **palatial**.

In this sentence, you understand that Brad Pitt's house is large and beautiful. Looking at the bold word, you can guess it is spelled like the word *palace*. So, here you can connect Brad Pitt's house and a palace. So, you can understand that his house is **as large and as beautiful as a palace**.

b. Slavery was **abolished** in the U.S. after the Civil War.

In this sentence, you can use what you already know about the world today. We know that slavery is unlawful in this era. A word similar to **unlawful** is *banned* or *outlawed*.

c. Francis' mother gets **anxious** when she stays outside after curfew.

In this sentence, you understand that Francis has a curfew, and if she does not stick to it, her mother is filled with negative emotions. A word similar to anxious is *nervous*.

Let us look at the following excerpt from *The Secret Garden* by Frances Hogsdon Burnett (1910).

When Mary Lennox was sent to Misselthwaite Manor to live with her uncle everybody said she was the most **disagreeable-looking** child ever seen. It was true, too. She had a little thin face and a little thin body, thin light hair and a sour **expression**. Her hair was yellow, and her face was yellow because she had been born in India and had always been ill in one way or another. Her father had held a position under the English Government and had always been busy and ill himself, and her mother had been a great beauty who cared only to go to parties and **amuse** herself with **gay** people.

This passage has some words that may be unfamiliar to you. We will look at them one by one.

1. **disagreeable-looking**

You can break down this word in the following way: **dis-agree-able-look-ing.** We know the word **agree** means to have "the same opinion about something." The word **look** has several meanings, but in this context, it refers to the "physical features of the child." The word **able** means "having considerable skills, proficiency or intelligence," while **dis-** is a Latin word that expresses negation or "not." Thus, you can understand that Mary's **features do not match that of a common "beautiful child."**

2. **expression**

You can break down the word in the following way: **express-ion.** We know the word **express** means "showing one's feelings." The word before this one is **sour,** which means "expressing distaste." Therefore, you can understand that Mary's face showed **a feeling of dislike**.

3. **amuse**

Mary's mother likes to go to parties. Therefore, you can understand that this word is a positive term that relates to the **feeling of being around people who are enjoying themselves**. A similar word to this is *entertain*.

4. **gay**

Similar to point number 3, this word has been used to refer to the people with whom Mary's mother likes to be. Today, the word **gay** can be used to refer to people within the lesbian, gay, bisexual, and trans (LGBT+) community, but it also describes a **light-hearted** and **carefree** attitude.

EXERCISE 2

Read the rest of the excerpt and fill in the spaces with alternate words using the following options:

ill, nurse, baby, madam, distressed

She had not wanted a little girl at all, and when Mary was born she handed her over to the care of an **Ayah** (_____), who was made to understand that if she wished to please the **Mem Sahib** (_____) she must keep the child out of sight as much as possible. So when she was a **sickly** (_____), **fretful** (_____), ugly little baby she was kept out of the way, and when she became a sickly, fretful, **toddling** (_____) thing she was kept out of the way also.

PRACTICE EXERCISE

Circle the word from the multiple-choice options that has a similar meaning to the one in bold.

1. When we went to the restaurant, we were offered a variety of **beverages**, like milk and iced tea.

    a. bread
    b. silverware
    c. drinks
    d. menus

2. **Pedestrians** should be attentive when crossing the street.

    a. crosswalks
    b. walkers
    c. stoplights
    d. parrots

3. I had to wear a cast for three months after I **fractured** my arm while trampolining.

    a. rested
    b. broke
    c. avoided
    d. looked at

4. Lance was asked to **exhibit** his award-winning science project during Parents' Night.

    a. lose
    b. eat
    c. trade
    d. show

5. Laila went for a swim. She regretted jumping into the pool without checking. The **frigid** water made her teeth chatter.

    a. cold
    b. clean
    c. green
    d. warm

6. After the rainstorm, the rainbow lit up the sky with **vivid** colors.

    a. dark
    b. funny
    c. bright
    d. normal

7. The following is an excerpt from *The Innocence of Father Brown* by G. K. Chesterton (1911). Using the text as a clue, fill in each blank with a word or phrase that would make sense using the following options:

landscape, should, miracles, accidentally, human, expressed

The most incredible thing about _____ is that they happen. A few clouds in heaven do come together into the staring shape of one _____ eye. A tree does stand up in the _____ of a doubtful journey in the exact and elaborate shape of a note of interrogation. I have seen both these things myself within the last few days. Nelson does die in the instant of victory: and a man named Williams does quite _____ murder a man named Williamson: it sounds like a sort of infanticide. In short, there is in life an element of elfin coincidence which people reckoning on the prosaic may perpetually miss. As it has been well _____ in the paradox of Poe, wisdom _____ reckon on the unforeseen.

8. Break down the following words and identify the root word, the prefix and the suffix.

WORD	PREFIX	ROOT WORD	SUFFIX
Telephone			
Translation			
Nonsense			
Creation			
Inscribe			
Loveable			
Autograph			

9. Read the following excerpt from *Dracula* by Bram Stoker (1897).

*When I found that I was a prisoner, a sort of wild feeling came over me. I **rushed** up and down the stairs, trying every door and peering out of every window I could find but after a little the **conviction** of my helplessness overpowered all other feelings. When I look back after a few hours, I think I must have been mad for the time, for I behaved much as a rat does in a trap. When, however, the conviction had come to me that I was **helpless**, I sat down quietly—as quietly as I have ever done anything in my life—and began to think over what was best to be done. I am thinking still, and as yet have come to no definite conclusion. Of one thing only am I certain: that it is no use making my ideas known to the Count. He knows well that I am **imprisoned**: and as he has done it himself, and has **doubtless** his own motives for it, he would only deceive me if I trusted him fully with the facts. So far as I can see, my only plan will be to keep my knowledge and my fears to myself, and my eyes open.*

What do the words in bold mean? Discuss the meaning with a classmate.

a. rushed: _____

b. conviction: _____

c. helpless: _____

d. imprisoned: _____

e. doubtless: _____

REFLECTION ON LEARNING

Answer the following reflection questions, and feel free to discuss your responses with your teacher or classmate.

- What reading idea or strategy did you learn from this section?

- What new concepts did you learn?

- What methods did you work on in this section?

- What aspect of this section is still not 100 percent clear for you?

- What do you want your teacher to know?

LESSON 3

TYPES OF TEXT STRUCTURES AND LINKING WORDS

Writers arrange their sentences in several ways to add flavor to their texts. A text that only uses the same sentence structure can be boring. In this lesson, we will look at four types of text structures: <u>cause and effect</u>, <u>compare and contrast</u>, <u>sequence and chronological order</u>, and <u>problem and solution</u>.

Cause and Effect

This type of text structure talks about why something happened (the cause) and what occurred because of it happening (the effect). Below are examples of sentences that are arranged in this way:

1.   Paula missed the bus (**cause**). She was late for a meeting (**effect**).
2.   It rained heavily last night (**cause**). The dam burst (**effect**).

The cause can also come before the effect:

1.   We ran out of gas (**effect**). We forgot to fill the tank before we left (**cause**).
2.   A tree started to burn (**effect**). Lightning had struck the tree (**cause**).
3.   The cake burned (**effect**). The oven was too hot (**cause**).

The sentences above are too short. To fix this, we can use <u>linking words</u> to join them:

1.   Paula missed the bus **and** was late for a meeting.
2.   It rained heavily last night rain **causing** the dam to burst.
3.   We ran out of gas **because** we forgot to fill the tank before we left.
4.   The tree started to burn **because** lightning had struck it.
5.   The cake burned **because** the oven was too hot.

EXERCISE 1

Write down what you think the cause and effect are in these sentences. Compare with a classmate.

1.   The horses were thirsty because it was very hot outside.

   Cause: _____

   Effect: _____

2.   Karen watched as the pot rattled on the stove because it had too much water.

   Cause: _____

   Effect: _____

Compare and Contrast

This type of text structure is useful when looking for differences and similarities between two things, peoples or events. Comparative texts look at the similarities while contrasting texts look at the differences. Some common linking words used in these types of texts include the following:

- as well as
- likewise
- otherwise

17

- meanwhile
- like
- just as
- instead
- however
- likewise
- contrarily

- too
- in comparison
- is similar to
- in the same way
- in contrast
- on the contrary
- although

- even though
- on the other hand
- as opposed to
- whereas
- in spite of
- both
- but

Let's take a look at some examples:

TYPE OF SENTENCE	SENTENCE	LINKING WORD	FINAL SENTENCE
Compare	Kennedy has long hair. Chandler has long hair.	**both**	**Both** Kennedy and Chandler have long hair.
Contrast	I am 12 years old. My brother is 2 years older.	**while**	**While** I am 12 years old, my brother is 2 years older.
Contrast	Trevor can jog 12 miles without stopping. I can only jog 7 miles without stopping.	**however**	Trevor can jog 12 miles without stopping; **however,** I can only jog for 7 miles.
Compare	I ordered chicken. I was served chicken.	**and**	I ordered chicken **and** was served chicken.
Compare	Amy has a good fashion sense. Grace has a good fashion sense.	**like**	**Like** Amy, Grace has a good fashion sense.
Contrast	It rained heavily last night. I walked to school.	**Despite**	I walked to school despite the heavy rain last night.

EXERCISE 2

Join the following sentences using appropriate linking words. Compare with a classmate.

1. I eat meat.
   My partner is a vegetarian.   _____

2. Carlos got an A in math.
   Carlos is doing well in other subjects.   _____

Sequence and Chronological Order

The order of events is essential to understating a piece of text. Whether it is fictional or nonfictional, every text has a beginning, a middle and an end. These three parts help readers follow the thoughts of the characters or the writer.

Read the following excerpt from an article titled "Exploration of the Americas" by Kerry Dunne.

*The historical details of European exploration of the Americas are many, and difficult to summarize. There is archaeological evidence of Viking exploration and temporary settlement in Eastern Canada and New England **around the year 1000**. Unconfirmed tales of Irish, African, and Polynesian exploration of the Americas **prior to 1492** also exist. But, without a doubt, the onslaught of European colonization **began in 1492** with the arrival of Christopher Columbus, and quickly accelerated as the Spanish claimed land in the Caribbean, Central America, Mexico, and South America, the French claimed land in the Caribbean and the central and northern portions of North America, and the British claimed land in what is today the eastern United States as well as Canada.*

From the above excerpt, you can understand the following things:

   a.   The story is about evidence of the exploration of the Americas.
   b.   Around year 1,000, Vikings might have explored and had a temporary settlement in Eastern Canada and New England.
   c.   Before 1492, there are unconfirmed tales of Irish, African, and Polynesian exploration.
   d.   The onslaught of European colonization began in 1492.
   e.   Christopher Columbus arrived in the Americas in 1492.
   f.   The Spanish, French, and British laid claim to some parts of the Americas.
   g.   The Spanish claimed the Caribbean, Central America, Mexico, and South America.
   h.   The French claimed the Caribbean and some parts of North America.
   i.   The British claimed the eastern side of the U.S. and Canada.

Read the following excerpt from an article titled "Frank Lloyd Wright and Modern American Architecture" by Ella Howard.

*Frank Lloyd Wright is regarded by many as the greatest American architect. In his effort to develop an American style of architecture, he designed over 1,100 buildings. Wright is most noted for developing the distinctive Prairie School style of architecture. **Born in Wisconsin in 1867** to a **teacher and a minister/musician**, Wright grew up feeling a strong connection to nature. **He enrolled at the University of Wisconsin at Madison** to **study civil engineering** but **left school after two years** to begin work as an architect. Early in his career, **Wright had the chance to spend five years working for Louis Sullivan,** who was highly regarded for his work designing skyscrapers. Sullivan's belief that form follows function was highly influential on Wright as well as other architects.*

From the above excerpt, you can understand the following things:

   a.   The text is about Frank Lloyd Wright.
   b.   He was born in 1867.
   c.   His parents were a teacher and a minister/musician.
   d.   He enrolled at the University of Wisconsin at Madison.
   e.   He studied civil engineering at the University of Wisconsin at Madison.
   f.   He dropped out of University of Wisconsin two years after enrolling.
   g.   Early in his career, he got the chance to spend five years working for Louis Sullivan.

EXERCISE 3

Read the following excerpt from *The Secret Garden* by Frances Hodgson Burnett (1910) and **put the story's events into the correct sequence.** Compare with a classmate.

> *One day, the robin remembered that when he himself had been made to learn to fly by his parents he had done much the same sort of thing. He had taken short flights of a few yards and then had been obliged to rest. So it occurred to him that this boy was learning to fly—or rather to walk. He mentioned this to his mate and when he told her that the Eggs would probably conduct themselves in the same way after they were fledged, she was quite comforted and even became eagerly interested and derived great pleasure from watching the boy over the edge of her nest—though she always thought that the Eggs would be much cleverer and learn more quickly. But then she said indulgently that humans were always more clumsy and slow than Eggs and most of them never seemed really to learn to fly at all. You never met them in the air or on tree-tops.*

_____ The robin mentioned to his friend that he observed a boy learning to walk like how he learned how to fly.

_____ The robin's friend says that humans are clumsy.

_____ The robin thinks her Eggs are cleverer than the boy.

_____ The robin remembered taking short flights of a few yards.

Problem and Solution

With this structure, writers present a problem that needs to be solved. A problem can be between individuals or groups, or it might be with something going on in the world. A problem might even occur with just one person. Let us take a look at some problem-and-solution sentences.

1. I tried to get Gale's attention at the train station, but my voice was no match for the rush-hour chaos **(problem).** Instead, I decided to text my question even though he was standing near me **(solution).**

From the above sentence, you understand that the character's voice was **too quiet** for Gale to hear. The problem was the **noisiness at the train station due to rush hour**. The character's solution was to **text** Gale her question.

2. Tee's baby had a cold that was causing her sleepless nights **(problem).** She tried a few home remedies, but nothing was working. She had to take the baby to the pediatrician to find out what was wrong **(solution).**

From the above sentence, you understand that Tee's baby's cold is causing her sleepless nights. The problem is the **baby's cold**. The solution is to **go to the pediatrician** to find out what is wrong.

3. "Get in here right now! How could you stay out so late?" Mother yelled across the street **(problem).** "The buses were delayed because of an accident on the highway," I said **(solution).**

From the above sentence, you understand that the character's mother is angry that her child got home late. The problem is the **lateness of the hour**. The solution is that Mother was given an **explanation** about what happened.

Let us take a look at how poems can also have this type of text structure. Read the following excerpt (stanzas 7 to 10) from the poem *Phantasmagoria and Other Poems* by Lewis Carroll (1911).

There is an insect that people avoid
(Whence is derived the verb 'to flee').
Where have you been by it most annoyed?
In lodgings by the Sea.

If you like your coffee with sand for dregs,
A decided hint of salt in your tea,
And a fishy taste in the very eggs—
By all means choose the Sea.

And if, with these dainties to drink and eat,
You prefer not a vestige of grass or tree,
And a chronic state of wet in your feet,
Then—I recommend the Sea.

For I have friends who dwell by the coast—
Pleasant friends they are to me!
It is when I am with them I wonder most
That anyone likes the Sea.

From the above poem, you can understand that the poet mentions several issues, and offers the solution: "the Sea." This poem focuses on offering "the Sea" as the solution to a problem.

EXERCISE 4

Can you identify two problems the poet has talked about?

1. _____

2. _____

PRACTICE EXERCISE

Read the following excerpt from an article titled "The Columbian Exchange" by Jamie Lathan. Answer the questions that follow and compare with a classmate.

Historical evidence proves that there were interactions between Europe and the Americas before Christopher Columbus's voyage in 1492. But Columbus's contact precipitated a large, impactful, and lastingly significant transfer of animals, crops, people groups, cultural ideas and microorganisms between the two worlds. In 1493, for example, on his second voyage, Columbus brought horses, dogs, pigs, cattle, chickens, sheep, and goats to the "new" world. Later in the 1530s, the Spanish conquistador and explorer, Francisco Pizarro, saw the potato in the Andes of South America and brought this crop to Europe. Bacteria and viruses, as well technological and cultural ideas, moved between the hemispheres, and Europeans forcibly transported enslaved people from Africa to the Americas to provide free labor. These transfers had a monumental impact on the development of our modern world. Alfred Crosby, who wrote an important 1972 book called The Columbian Exchange: Biological and Cultural Consequences of 1492, *asserts that the commingling of plants, animals, and bacteria resulting from the Columbian Exchange is one of the most important ecological events in human history.*

1. When did Christopher Columbus first voyage? _____

2. What was the effect of Columbus' second voyage? _____

   _____

3. Who wrote *The Columbian Exchange: Biological and Cultural Consequences of 1492?*

   _____

4. Who brought the potato to Europe? _____

5. Using the passage above, how did slavery begin?

   _____

Below are two excerpts written by Charles Dickens in *Great Expectations (1861)* and *A Christmas Carol (1843)*. These excerpts describe old men but are written in a different way.

A fearful man, all in coarse gray, with a great iron on his leg. A man with no hat, and with broken shoes, and with an old rag tied round his head. A man who had been soaked in water, and smothered in mud, and lamed by stones, and cut by flints, and stung by nettles, and torn by briars: who limped, and shivered, and glared, and growled: and whose teeth chattered in his head as he seized me by the chin.	*Oh! but he was a tight-fisted hand at the grindstone, Scrooge! a squeezing, wrenching, grasping, scraping, clutching, covetous, old sinner! Hard and sharp as flint, from which no steel had ever struck out generous fire: secret, and self-contained, and solitary as an oyster. The cold within him froze his old features, nipped his pointed nose, shriveled his cheek, stiffened his gait: made his eyes red, his thin lips blue: and spoke out shrewdly in his grating voice. A frosty rime was on his head, and on his eyebrows, and his wiry chin. He carried his own low temperature always about with him: he iced his office in the dog-days: and didn't thaw it one degree at Christmas.*
Great Expectations by Charles Dickens	*A Christmas Carol by Charles Dickens*

6. List at least two differences in the way that Dickens describes the old men. Compare with a classmate.

   _____

   _____

7. Write a paragraph summarizing what you have found about the men.

   _____

   _____

REFLECTION ON LEARNING

Answer the following reflection questions, and feel free to discuss your responses with your teacher or classmate.

- What reading idea or strategy did you learn from this section?

- What new concepts did you learn?

- What methods did you work on in this section?

- What aspect of this section is still not 100 percent clear for you?

- What do you want your teacher to know?

LESSON 4
USING BACKGROUND KNOWLEDGE

Do you remember your favorite vacation? Or the first time you traveled for a holiday? When reading, we can use what we already know to understand the text better. These life experiences build and form our background knowledge. By the end of this lesson, you will be able to use background knowledge to understand the text you are reading. We will explore <u>text-to-self</u>, <u>text-to-text</u> and <u>text-to-world</u> connections.

Text-to-Self

We make *text-to-self* connections all the time, whether we are in formal or informal situations. When we attach these personal connections to the text we are reading, we better understand what the writer means. You can apply the following steps when making *picture-to-self* connections, too. Most times, we use the following phrases to connect with the text:

- My teacher used to…
- I act like that when…
- I remember…
- That's similar to…
- It's just like…
- That reminds me of…
- My brother acts just like that when…

Read this excerpt from an article titled "Powhatan People and the English at Jamestown" by Catherine Denial.

In 1607, a party of Englishmen landed in a place they called Virginia. They followed in the footsteps of Sir Walter Raleigh, who had visited Virginia (which, at the time, included North Carolina) with a party of settlers in 1585. The colony founded by Raleigh's party failed, weakened by lack of supplies and irregular contact with England. To the people who already lived in the area, this was the land of the Powhatan Confederacy, a vast regional network of allied communities living under the leadership of Wahunsenacah (also known as Powhatan).

You might make a **text-to-self connection** in the following way:

(When Raleigh's party failed due to lack of supplies.) **That is similar to when** I don't have money to buy art supplies to finish my painting. I love to paint, and it is a stress reliever. So when I do not have money to buy the supplies, I feel like I cannot do what relaxes me.

(When Raleigh's party failed due to irregular contact with England.) **My teacher used to** say that technology has more advantages than disadvantages, including being able to talk to people who are thousands of miles away from us.

Let us use the same steps to try and make a picture-to-self connection. Have a look at the following picture. What comes to mind when you look at it? Here are some ideas:

- **This reminds me of when** I was in the track team in high school. My track coach used to count down in reverse order. She said that it helps to keep runners attentive at the start of the track meet.

- **I state this when** I'm trying to motivate myself to do something I am scared to do. Just the other day, I repeated this just before I dived into the pool.

Now it's your turn. Make a connection with the picture.

Text-to-Text

Text-to-text connections involve making a connection between two or more texts you are reading. With this type of connection, you try to find the similarities or differences between the texts, which makes it easier to understand the reading. You can apply the following steps when making <u>picture-to-picture</u> connections as well.

Let us take a look at the following excerpts:

In To Kill a Mockingbird, *set in the deeply prejudiced South in the midst of the Great Depression, an adult Jean Louise "Scout" Finch tells her story of growing up in Maycomb, Alabama. Scout learns about prejudice and empathy as events unfold around her. Her father, Atticus Finch, is the court-appointed lawyer for Tom Robinson, a black man accused of rape. Lee takes the story straight from the headlines in the 1930s when the Scottsboro boys (nine young men) were falsely accused of raping two white women on a train. The social inequities of a small Southern town are brought to life through the innocent eyes of a young girl.*	*Maxine Hong Kingston's* The Woman Warrior: Memoirs of a Girlhood Among the Ghosts *(1976) weaves together elements from traditional Chinese folktales and incidents from the author's experiences or family stories in five interconnected chapters. These chapters follow the lives of several women while they lived in China and/or after immigration to the United States: Kingston, her mother Brave Orchid, and her aunts, Moon Orchid and No Name Woman. Kingston, a first-generation Chinese-American, was born in Stockton, California, in 1940.*
From an article titled "To Kill a Mockingbird by Harper Lee."	*From an article titled "The Woman Warrior by Maxine Hong Kingston."*

So, how can you make a connection between these two texts? Here are some ideas:

- The texts are commenting on novels.

- The stories in the texts are based on events that happened in the early to mid-1900s.

- The main characters are female.

EXERCISE 1

Let us use the same steps to try and make a picture-to-picture connection. Look at the pictures below:

What comes to mind when you look at them? What are the picture-to-picture connections here? Discuss with a classmate.

_____

_____

Text-to-World

Text-to-world connections are usually challenging to make and almost always have a negative tinge to them. Unfortunately, it's probably easier to remember the negative events in our lives. When reading, try to relate the text with a positive memory, if possible. You can apply the following steps when making picture-to-world connections, too.

Let's take a look at this excerpt from *None Other Gods* by Robert Hugh Benson (1910).

> *Somehow or another, the sense of sordidness, which presently began to affect Frank so profoundly, descended on him for the first time that night. He had managed, by his very solitariness hitherto, to escape it so far. It had been possible to keep up a kind of pose so far: to imagine the adventure in the light of a very much prolonged and very realistic picnic. But with this other man the thing became impossible. It was tolerable to wash one's own socks: it was not so tolerable to see another man's socks hung up on the peeling mantelpiece a foot away from his own head, and to see two dirty ankles, not his own, emerging from crazy boots. The Major, too, presently, when he grew a trifle maudlin over his own sorrows, began to call him "Frankie," and "my boy," and somehow it mattered, from a man with the Major's obvious record. Frank pulled himself up only just in time to prevent a retort when it first happened, but it was not the slightest use to be resentful. The thing had to be borne. And it became easier when it occurred to him to regard the Major as a study: it was even interesting to hear him give himself away, yet all with a pompous appearance of self-respect, and to recount his first meeting with Gertie, now asleep upstairs.*

What connections can you make between the text you are reading and what is happening in the world today? Here are some thoughts:

- In the recent past, COVID-19 led to government mandates for us to be on lockdown. Though we were in isolation, some of us were able to refocus ourselves and learn new skills.
- We also started to work online and realized the benefits of technology.

EXERCISE 2

Let us use the same steps to try to make a picture-to-world connection. Have a look at the following picture. Can you make any text-to-world connections with the picture? Discuss with a partner.

_____

_____

_____

Final Thoughts

When making any type of connection, always remember to think about
- Whether the text reminds you of an event in your life.
- What you know about the topic.
- How you can use life experiences to understand and predict the message in the text.
- What the article tells you about the world.
- Whether you agree or disagree with the writer, and why.

PRACTICE EXERCISE

1. Read the excerpt from *The Secret Garden* by Frances Hodgson Burnett (1910) below and answer the questions that follow.

> But when Colin held forth under his tree, old Ben fixed devouring eyes on him and kept them there. He looked him over with critical affection. It was not so much the lecture which interested him as the legs which looked straighter and stronger each day, the boyish head which held itself up so well, the once sharp chin and hollow cheeks which had filled and rounded out and the eyes which had begun to hold the light he remembered in another pair. Sometimes when Colin felt Ben's earnest gaze meant that he was much impressed he wondered what he was reflecting on and once when he had seemed quite entranced he questioned him.

   a. Make three text-to-self connections using the following phrases:

      i. I act like Colin when I _____

       _____

     ii. Ben reminds me of _____

       _____

    iii. This excerpt reminds me of _____

       _____

   b. Make three text-to-world connections:

      _____

      _____

      _____

2. The following is a photograph of President Lyndon B. Johnson signing the Voting Rights Act, 1965.

   a. What text-to-self connection can you make with the picture?

      _____

      _____

   b. What text-to-world connection can you make from the picture?

      _____

      _____

3. Read the following excerpts and answer the questions that follow.

It was a queer sort of place—a gable-ended old house, one side palsied as it were, and leaning over sadly. It stood on a sharp bleak corner, where that tempestuous wind Euroclydon kept up a worse howling than ever it did about poor Paul's tossed craft. Euroclydon, nevertheless, is a mighty pleasant zephyr to any one in-doors, with his feet on the hob quietly toasting for bed.

Moby-Dick Or, The Whale by Herman Melville (1851)

The first consideration was of great moment to me: my trade was a saddler, and as my dealings were chiefly not by a shop or chance trade, but among the merchants trading to the English colonies in America, so my effects lay very much in the hands of such. I was a single man, 'tis true, but I had a family of servants whom I kept at my business: had a house, shop, and warehouses filled with goods: and, in short, to leave them all as things in such a case must be left (that is to say, without any overseer or person fit to be trusted with them), had been to hazard the loss not only of my trade, but of my goods, and indeed of all I had in the world.

A Journal of the Plague Year by Daniel Defoe (1722)

a. Write down one difference in the narrators of the two excerpts.

_____

_____

b. Can you make two text-to-world connections with *A Journal of the Plague Year* by Daniel Defoe (1722)?

_____

_____

c. Can you make two text-to-self connection with *Moby-Dick Or, The Whale* by Herman Melville (1851)?

_____

_____

4. Look at the image below. What text-to-self connection can you make starting with the phrase below? Compare with a classmate.

This reminds me of when _____

REFLECTION ON LEARNING

Answer the following reflection questions, and feel free to discuss your responses with your teacher or classmate.

- What reading idea or strategy did you learn from this section?

- What new concepts did you learn?

- What methods did you work on in this section?

- What aspect of this section is still not 100 percent clear for you?

- What do you want your teacher to know?

LESSON 5

UNDERSTANDING FIGURATIVE LANGUAGE

Just as a painter uses brushes and paint to create an image, a writer uses figurative language to enhance the meaning of their work. Writers use this technique to bring their writings to life, allowing the reader to create and visualize images in their head. By the end of this lesson, you will learn about five forms of figurative language: symbolism, hyperbole, alliteration, simile and metaphor.

Symbolism

Symbolism is the use of a single word or an object to represent a whole idea. The actual meaning of something is different from the meaning the writer is trying to convey.

Let's look at a couple of examples:

3. Red symbolizes love.
4. Violets represent shyness.
5. A dog represents loyalty and faith.
6. Spring is used for happiness and new beginnings.
7. Snow represents purity.
8. Green represents nature.
9. A sunflower represents opportunities.
10. An anemone (a type of flower) is used for anticipation.
11. A thunderstorm is used for hostility.
12. Lions represent bravery and courage.
13. Owls represent wisdom or intuition.

To determine whether an object is being used symbolically in a story, consider if it appears multiple times or in essential passages of the text. Let us take a look at a couple of sentences:

1. The rebels raised **a white flag** to negotiate.

In this sentence, "a white flag" symbolizes making peace with the enemy.

2. My mom has **a sixth sense like an owl**.

In this sentence, the symbolism is in the words "a sixth sense like an owl." They have been used to symbolize wisdom.

3. Laila **works like an ox**.

In this sentence, the symbolism is "works like an ox." It has been used to symbolize that Laila has worked hard.

4. **Life is a rollercoaster.**

This is an example of a metaphor that has symbolism. This is symbolic because it indicates that there will be ups and downs in life.

5. In his vows, Charlie said his bride is **his rock.**

In this sentence, the symbolism is "his rock." This is symbolic because it signifies his wife is strong and dependable.

I met a traveler from an antique land
Who said: Two vast and trunkless legs of stone
Stand in the desert. Near them, on the sand,
Half sunk, a shattered visage lies, whose frown,
And wrinkled lip, and sneer of cold command,
Tell that its sculptor well those passions read
Which yet survive, stamped on these lifeless things,
The hand that mocked them, and the heart that fed:
And on the pedestal these words appear:
"My name is Ozymandias, king of kings:
Look on my works, ye Mighty, and despair!"
Nothing beside remains. Round the decay
Of that colossal wreck, boundless and bare
The lone and level sands stretch far away.

Ozymandias by Percy Bysshe Shelley (1818)

In the above poem, symbolism transforms the **half-sunken monument** into a representation of the passage of time. In the final lines, the poem shows two very different symbols: the fallen statue, greatly diminished from its former size, and the huge, barren and unchanging desert. The statue of Ozymandias shows man's mortality and smallness in the face of time and nature.

EXERCISE 1

Can you guess what the following words and phrases symbolize?

1. Flesh: _____

2. He turned **green** when found a wallet: _____

3. A dove with an olive branch: _____

Hyperboles

With hyperboles, a writer creates exaggerated descriptions. Exaggeration is used for effect and emphasizes thoughts. Look at these examples:

1. Trevor commented that he has **millions of papers** to grade this weekend.
2. Jallie thought her beauty **shone as brightly as all the stars in the heavens**.
3. "I moved **heaven and earth** to buy this face cream," Molly boasted.
4. I'm giving it **110 percent of my effort**.
5. **Everybody knows** the lyrics to the anthem.
6. Larry was such a big baby that his parents had to use bed sheets for diapers.
7. My bedroom roof **rose up and down** to the rhythm of my brother's music next door.
8. The dog **was so dirty** that it had a tomato plant growing on its back.

Hyperboles can also be used in music. Take a look at the following song.

You told me you love me
Why did you leave me all alone
Now you tell me you need me
When you call me on the phone
Girl, I refuse
You must have me confused with some other guy
The bridges were burned
Now it's your turn to cry
Cry me a river (go on and just)
Cry me a river (go on and just)
Cry me a river (baby, go on and just)
Cry me a river

"Cry Me a River" by Justin Timberlake (2002)

From the above excerpt, you can understand that the singer uses hyperbole to emphasize the emotions related to breaking up with someone. You can think about it as a passive-aggressive way of saying that it is now his ex-lover's turn to suffer because of breaking his heart.

EXERCISE 2

Strumming my pain with his fingers
Singing my life with his words
Killing me softly with his song
Killing me softly with his song
Telling my whole life with his words
Killing me softly with his song

"Killing Me Softly" by Roberta Flack (1973)

From the above excerpt, you can understand that the singer uses hyperbole to emphasize her feelings because of a man she met. The entire verse is an exaggeration, but it matches the intended meaning of the song. Can you explain what the following hyperboles mean? Discuss with a classmate.

1. I am so tired I could sleep for a hundred years. _____

2. The hare had ears a mile long. _____

Alliteration

This literary device uses the repetition of sounds at the beginning of nearby words. Writers use this as a tool to create rhythm and emphasize certain words and concepts. Companies use this technique to create catchy names and slogans. Here are some examples:

- Dunkin' Donuts
- PayPal
- Best Buy
- Coca-Cola
- The Scotch and Sirloin

- Life Lock
- Park Place
- American Apparel
- American Airlines

- Chuckee Cheese's
- Bed Bath & Beyond
- Krispy Kreme

Tongue twisters also use this type of technique. Look at these examples:

- Peter Piper picked a peck of pickled peppers.
- She sells seashells by the seashore.
- How much wood would a woodchuck chuck if a woodchuck could chuck wood?
- I never smelt a smell that smelt like that smell I smelt.
- Red lorry, blue lorry, yellow lorry, green lorry.

Take a look at some other examples:

- Tanya took a walk in the evening. The **ch**illing autumn almost **ch**opped her apart.
- The **c**aptain **k**ept most of his fielders within the circle.
- As soon as Manny reached the station, he **c**aught a **c**old.
- His **f**aithful **f**riend now calls him Brutus because of his recent betrayal.
- The **l**ion **l**icked the wounds of indignation after his prey was snatched by the hyenas.
- The ship **s**ailed and **s**ank like the Titanic.
- The **s**cholar **s**uffered from the worst **s**ort of narcissism.

EXERCISE 3

Can you identify examples of alliteration in this passage? Discuss with a classmate.

> By this time, now and then sheering to one side or the other to avoid a reef, but still hugging the wind and the land, we had got round Iona and begun to come alongside Mull. The tide at the tail of the land ran very strong, and threw the brig about. Two hands were put to the helm, and Hoseason himself would sometimes lend a help: and it was strange to see three strong men throw their weight upon the tiller, and it (like a living thing) struggle against and drive them back. This would have been the greater danger had not the sea been for some while free of obstacles. Mr. Riach, besides, announced from the top that he saw clear water ahead.
>
> ———
>
> Excerpt from Kidnapped by Robert Louis Stevenson (1886).

EXERCISE 4

Read the following excerpt from "The Rime of the Ancient Mariner" by Samuel Taylor Coleridge (1834).

Behemoth biggest born of earth upheaved
His vastness: Fleeced the flocks and bleating rose,
As plants: Ambiguous between sea and land
The river-horse, and scaly crocodile.

Can you identify examples of alliteration in the above passage?

Similes

Similes are one of the most common and user-friendly forms of figurative language. They are used to compare two different things using the words "like" or "as." Take a look at some examples:

1. The food was **as hot as lava**!

In this sentence, the food is described as the same temperature as lava.

2. Lilly's voice is **as pretty as a bird's song**.

In this sentence, the simile likens Lilly's voice to the sound of a bird singing.

3. Paul thought that sleeping in my bed was **like floating on a cloud**.

In this sentence, the simile likens the comfort of the bed to the fluffiness of a cloud.

4. His eyes **darkened like night**.

In this sentence, the simile shows that the character's expression is a dark one.

5. He looked **as happy as a cat** in a sunbeam.

In this sentence, the simile likens the character's happiness to that of a cat's.

You can also replace a simple adjective with a simile to make a stronger impression. Below are some examples:

1. The girl was sad.
    The girl was as sad as a little girl who had dropped her ice cream cone.
2. The essay was difficult.
    The essay was as difficult as brain surgery.

3. Our bedroom is messy.
    Our bedroom is as messy as a toddler's.
4. Frankie's burrito is spicy.
    Frankie's burrito is as spicy as a jalapeno pepper.

Similes are popular in poems, too. Let's take a look at an excerpt from 'The Base Stealer' by Robert Francis (1976). The underlined words are similes.

> *"Poised between going on and back, pulled*
> *Both ways taut <u>like a tightrope-walker</u>,*
> *Fingertips pointing the opposites,*
> *Now bouncing tiptoe <u>like a dropped ball</u>*
> *Or a kid skipping rope, come on, come on,*
> *Running a scattering of steps sidewise,*
> *How he teeters, skitters, tingles, teases..."*

EXERCISE 5

What are the similes in these sentences? Compare your answers with a classmate's.

1. The boy drinks like a fish at the water fountain. _____
2. The runner slithered like a snake across the finish line. _____
3. My friend is as thin as a rail. _____
4. The man fights like a lion on the soccer field. _____

Metaphor

The metaphor is very similar to the simile. The primary difference between a metaphor and a simile is the use of the words "like" or "as" in similes to create a comparison between two different things. In a metaphor, you do not use those words. Here are a few examples:

1. My **mother** is **both the queen and the president**.

In this sentence, the metaphor compares the character's mother to a queen and president.

2. The **day off** from school **was a golden ticket to freedom.**

In this sentence, the metaphor compares the day off with a golden ticket. This is done to emphasize the day off as freeing.

3. His **solution** to the problem was just a **band-aid**.

In this sentence, the solution is compared to a band-aid. In other words, the solution is temporary.

4. The long afternoons of detention **were a prison sentence**.
In this sentence, the metaphor refers to the detention as a prison sentence.

5. The **children's laughter** was **music to my ears.**
In this sentence, the metaphor refers to the children's laughter as music.

It can be challenging to understand the meaning of metaphors, but you can use clues within the sentences to find out the meaning. Let's look at some examples:

1. My life is a dream come true!
In this metaphor, we can break down the sentence in the following way: "My life is going very well. I'm getting everything I've always wanted."

2. His hair is an ocean of waves.
In this metaphor, we can break down the sentence in the following way: "His hair is curly with lots of waves."

3. A book is a key that unlocks your imagination.
In this metaphor, we can break down the sentence in the following way: "Reading books improves your ability to imagine things and be creative."

4. The music of her laughter filled the room.
In this metaphor, we can break down the sentence in the following way: "Her laughter was a pleasant sound in the room."

5. Her diary was her best friend, guarding her secrets quietly.
In this metaphor, we can break down the sentence in the following way: "Her secrets were safe because they were written in her diary, which could not talk."

Let us look at examples as used in music:

A tornado flew around my room before you came *Excuse the mess it made, it usually doesn't rain in* *Southern California much like Arizona* *My eyes don't shed tears, but, boy, they bawl* *---* *Thinking Bout You by Frank Ocean (2012)*	*Here, the singer uses the metaphor of a room as a representation of his life. By stating that "a tornado flew around his room," the singer is saying that his life was crazy, like a tornado, before his partner came into his life.*
When the morning comes *When we see what we've become* *In the cold light of day, we're a flame in the wind* *Not the fire that we've begun* *----* *"Happier" by Marshmello & Bastille (2018)*	*The writer uses the metaphor of a "flame in the wind" to describe the current state of their deteriorating relationship. In the next line, the writer states that their relationship used to be a "fire" expressing that their relationship is not where it used to be.*

EXERCISE 6

Look at the following lyrics from "Everything" by Michael Bublé (2007). What do you think the following lyrics mean? Discuss with a classmate.

You're a fallen star
You're the getaway car
You're the line in the sand
When I go too far
You're the swimming pool
On an August day
And you're the perfect thing to say

PRACTICE EXERCISE

1. Read the following excerpt from *Poems, Series 1* by Emily Dickinson.

Pink, small, and punctual,
Aromatic, low,
Covert in April,
Candid in May,

Dear to the moss,
Known by the knoll,
Next to the robin
In every human soul.

Bold little beauty,
Bedecked with thee,
Nature forswears
Antiquity.

a. What comes to mind when you think about the poem?

_____

b. List four examples of alliteration used in the poem.

_____

2. Read the following excerpt from *The Legend Of Sleepy Hollow* by Washington Irving (1820).

He was tall, but exceedingly lank, with narrow shoulders, long arms and legs, hands that <u>dangled a mile out of his sleeves</u>, feet that <u>might have served for shovels</u>, and his whole frame most loosely hung together. His head was small, and flat at top, with huge ears, large green glassy eyes, and a long snipe nose, so that it looked like a weather-cock perched upon his spindle neck to tell which way the wind blew. To see him striding along the profile of a hill on a windy day, with his clothes bagging and fluttering about him, one might have <u>mistaken him for the genius of famine descending upon the earth</u>, or <u>some scarecrow eloped from a cornfield</u>.

The underlined areas are hyperboles. What do you think they mean? Discuss with a classmate.

   a. *dangled a mile out of his sleeves:* _____

   _____

   b. *might have served for shovels:* _____

   _____

   c. *mistaken him for the genius of famine descending upon the earth:* _____

   _____

   d. *some scarecrow eloped from a cornfield:* _____

   _____

3. Read the following excerpt from Barack Obama's speech on the 50th Anniversary of the Selma March.

   > The American instinct that led these young men and women to pick up the torch and cross this bridge is the same instinct that moved patriots to choose revolution over tyranny. It's the same instinct that drew immigrants from across oceans and the Rio Grande: the same instinct that led women to reach for the ballot and workers to organize against an unjust status quo: the same instinct that led us to plant a flag at Iwo Jima and on the surface of the Moon.

   How has symbolism been used in this speech?

   _____

   _____

4. Finish the following sentences using a simile.

   a. The old bread was as dry as _____
   b. The yowling of the cat at night was like_____
   c. When she received the news, Jesse's face glowed like _____
   d. After eating a huge dinner, Pete's belly was round like _____
   e. Jennifer's bedroom was as messy as _____

5. "Cathy is as cute as a kitten" is an example of what two types of figurative language?
   _____

6. What is being compared in these metaphors? Compare with a classmate.

   a.   My dad was an angry beast when I brought home my poor report card.

   _____

   b.   The lion at the show was a funny clown because it would play with its food.

   _____

   c.   The teacher was a bear to deal with in class because he was so strict.

   _____

REFLECTION ON LEARNING

Answer the following reflection questions, and feel free to discuss your responses with your teacher or classmate.

- What reading idea or strategy did you learn from this section?

- What new concepts did you learn?

- What methods did you work on in this section?

- What aspect of this section is still not 100 percent clear for you?

- What do you want your teacher to know?

LESSON 6

UNDERSTANDING MAIN IDEAS AND FINDING EVIDENCE

The easiest way to identify the main idea of a text is to think about a summary of it, which depends on the genre and style of writing. The main idea can be found in any section of the text, particularly at the beginning or the end. Therefore, it is crucial to read all the paragraphs. As you read, look for supporting evidence for the main idea. In exam situations, you will answer many questions related to main ideas, evidence, supporting details and the author's purpose.

You can also understand the main idea from the images and the title of the text. These two aspects can contain the clues that will allow you to figure out what the writer means.

Take a look at a couple of short paragraphs as examples.

Example 1

> *With this, Mrs. Rachel stepped out of the lane into the backyard of Green Gables. Very green and neat and precise was that yard, set about on one side with great patriarchal willows and the other with prim Lombardies. Not a stray stick nor stone was to be seen, for Mrs. Rachel would have seen it if there had been. Privately she was of the opinion that Marilla Cuthbert swept that yard over as often as she swept her house. One could have eaten a meal off the ground without over-brimming the proverbial peck of dirt.*
> _____
> *Excerpt from* Anne of Green Gables *by Lucy Maud Montgomery (1908).*

PART A: The main idea in this passage is that Green Gables' backyard was neat and clean.

PART B: The supporting evidence for this includes the following:
(a) There were no sticks scattered about.
(b) Marilla swept the yard as much as the house.
(c) The yard was so clean that someone could eat a meal off the ground.

Example 2

> *"There are more things to find out about in this house," he said to himself, "than all my family could find out in all their lives. I shall certainly stay and find out." He spent all that day roaming over the house. He nearly drowned himself in the bathtubs, put his nose into the ink on a writing table, and burned it on the end of the big man's cigar, for he climbed up in the big man's lap to see how writing was done. At nightfall he ran into Teddy's nursery to watch how kerosene lamps were lighted, and when Teddy went to bed, Rikki-tikki climbed up too. But he was a restless companion, because he had to get up and attend to every noise all through the night, and find out what made it. Teddy's mother and father came in, the last thing, to look at their boy, and Rikki-tikki was awake on the pillow. "I don't like that," said Teddy's mother. "He may bite the child." "He'll do no such thing," said the father. "Teddy's safer with that little beast than if he had a bloodhound to watch him. If a snake came into the nursery now—"*
> _____
> *Excerpt from* The Jungle Book: Rikki-Tikki-Tavi *by Rudyard Kipling (1894)*

PART A: The main idea in this passage is that the main character, Rikki-Tikki-Tavi, enjoys exploring his surroundings.

PART B: The supporting evidence for this includes the following:
(a) The character puts his nose in the ink.

(b) The character wants to know how kerosene lamps are lighted.

(c) The character got up during the night to investigate every noise.

PRACTICE EXERCISE

Even with eyes protected by the green spectacles, Dorothy and her friends were at first dazzled by the brilliancy of the wonderful City. The streets were lined with beautiful houses all built of green marble and studded everywhere with sparkling emeralds. They walked over a pavement of the same green marble, and where the blocks were joined together were rows of emeralds, set closely, and glittering in the brightness of the sun. The window panes were of green glass: even the sky above the City had a green tint, and the rays of the sun were green. There were many people--men, women, and children--walking about, and these were all dressed in green clothes and had greenish skins. They looked at Dorothy and her strangely assorted company with wondering eyes, and the children all ran away and hid behind their mothers when they saw the Lion: but no one spoke to them. Many shops stood in the street, and Dorothy saw that everything in them was green. Green candy and green popcorn were offered for sale, as well as green shoes, green hats, and green clothes of all sorts. At one place, a man was selling green lemonade, and when the children bought it, Dorothy could see that they paid for it with green pennies.

Excerpt The Wonderful Wizard of Oz by L. Frank Baum (1900).

1. a. The main idea in this passage is a description of the Emerald City.

    b. Write down three statements as supporting evidence.

_____

_____

_____

2. Read this poem from "Phantasmagoria and Other Poems: A Valentine" by Lewis Carroll (1911) and answer the questions below. Compare with a classmate.

And cannot pleasures, while they last,
Be actual unless, when past,
They leave us shuddering and aghast,
With anguish smarting?
And cannot friends be firm and fast,
And yet bear parting?

And must I then, at Friendship's call,
Calmly resign the little all
(Trifling, I grant, it is and small)

I have of gladness,
And lend my being to the thrall
Of gloom and sadness?

And think you that I should be dumb,
And full dolorum omnium,
Excepting when you choose to come
And share my dinner?
At other times be sour and glum
And daily thinner

a. What is the main idea in this poem?

_____

_____

b. What is your evidence?

_____

_____

c. Suggest an appropriate title.

_____

3. Read the following excerpt from *Little Women* by Louisa May Alcott (1869) and answer the questions that follow.

"A gloomy wood," according to the one playbill, was represented by a few shrubs in pots, green baize on the floor, and a cave in the distance. This cave was made with a clothes horse for a roof, bureaus for walls, and in it was a small furnace in full blast, with a black pot on it and an old witch bending over it. The stage was dark and the glow of the furnace had a fine effect, especially as real steam issued from the kettle when the witch took off the cover. A moment was allowed for the first thrill to subside, then Hugo, the villain, stalked in with a clanking sword at his side, a slouching hat, black beard, mysterious cloak, and the boots. After pacing to and from in much agitation, he struck his forehead, and burst out in a wild strain, singing of his hatred for Roderigo, his love for Zara, and his pleasing resolution to kill the one and win the other. The gruff tones of Hugo's voice, with an occasional shout when his feelings overcame him, were very impressive, and the audience applauded the moment he paused for breath. Bowing with the air of one accustomed to public praise, he stole to the cavern and ordered Hagar to come forth with a commanding, "What ho, minion! I need thee!"

a. What do you think is the main idea in this paragraph?

_____

_____

b. What is your supporting evidence?

_____

_____

c. Suggest an appropriate title (besides the current one).

_____

_____

4. Look at the image below.

a. What does the image tell you?_____

b. In a few words, write text to accompany this image.

_____

c. Can you suggest a title?_____

d. Can you make a picture-to-self connection? _____

REFLECTION ON LEARNING

Answer the following reflection questions, and feel free to discuss your responses with your teacher or classmate.

- What reading idea or strategy did you learn from this section?

- What new concepts did you learn?

- What methods did you work on in this section?

- What aspect of this section is still not 100 percent clear for you?

- What do you want your teacher to know?

LESSON 7

MINI-PRACTICE TEST

You have reached the mid-way point of this book. Have a go at this practice test to see how well you understand what you have learned so far. Discuss your answers with a classmate.

1. Rewrite the following sentences using a simile of your choice.

   a. The movie was exciting: _____.

   b. Jackie and Mason were brave: _____.

   c. The coat was wet: _____.

2. Look at these two pictures and answer the following questions.

   Title 1   Title 2

   a. Give these two images a title.

   Title 1: _____

   Title 2: _____

   b. Can you make three picture-to-picture connections with these images? Write three sentences to summarize the connection between the two pictures.

   _____

   _____

   _____

3. What do the following metaphors mean?

   a. Love is the dessert of life: _____

   _____

   b. My parents are the sturdy branches from which all of us flowers grow: _____

   _____

   c. Snowdrifts cover the city in sparkling diamonds: _____

   _____

   d. The classroom is a magic box full of tricks to discover: _____

   _____

4. Read the following passage from *The Velveteen Rabbit* by Margery Williams (1922).

> For a long time, he lived in the toy cupboard or on the nursery floor, and no one thought very much about him. He was **naturally** shy, and being only made of **velveteen**, some of the more **expensive** toys quite **snubbed** him. The mechanical toys were very **superior**, and looked down upon everyone else: they were full of modern ideas, and pretended they were real. The model boat, who had lived through two **seasons** and lost most of his paint, caught the tone from them and never missed an **opportunity** of **referring to** his rigging in **technical** terms. The Rabbit could not claim to be a model of anything, for he didn't know that real rabbits **existed**: he thought they were all stuffed with sawdust like himself, and he understood that **sawdust** was quite **out-of-date** and should never be mentioned in modern circles. Even Timothy, the jointed wooden lion, who was made by the disabled soldiers, and should have had broader views, put on airs, and pretended he was connected with Government. Between them all the poor little Rabbit was made to feel himself very insignificant and commonplace, and the only person who was kind to him at all was the Skin Horse.

Match the words with their meanings.

_____	I. naturally	A. talking about
_____	II. velveteen	B. chance
_____	III. expensive	C. old-fashioned
_____	IV. snubbed	D. soft wood chips
_____	V. superior	E. times of the year
_____	VI. seasons	F. soft cloth
_____	VII. opportunity	G. as expected
_____	VIII. referring to	H. lived
_____	IX. technical	I. special knowledge
_____	X. existed	J. ignored
_____	XI. sawdust	K. cost a lot of money
_____	XII. out-of-date	L. stuck up

5. Write the root word and its meaning for each of the words below.

	WHOLE WORD	ROOT WORD	MEANING OF ROOT WORD
a.	Wonderment		
b.	Development		
c.	Unlikable		
d.	Government		
e.	Sincerity		

6. Fill out the following passage with the most suitable words from the following options. The excerpt is from 'Anthem' by Ayn Rand (1937).

wax, scholars, hundred, rain, questions, earth

All the great modern inventions come from the Home of the Scholars, such as the newest one, which was found only a _____ years ago, of how to make candles from _____ and string: also, how to make glass, which is put in our windows to protect us from the _____. To find these things, the _____ must study the _____ and learn from the rivers, from the sands, from the winds and the rocks. And if we went to the Home of the Scholars, we could learn from these also. We could ask _____ of these, for they do not forbid questions.

REFLECTION ON LEARNING

Answer the following reflection questions, and feel free to discuss your responses with your teacher or classmate.

- What reading idea or strategy did you learn from this section?

- What new concepts did you learn?

- What methods did you work on in this section?

- What aspect of this section is still not 100 percent clear for you?

- What do you want your teacher to know?

LESSON 8

USING K-W-L CHARTS TO UNDERSTAND LONG PASSAGES

Have you heard of K-W-L charts? Do you know what the acronym stands for? The "KWL" stands for "What do you **Know**?", "What do you **Want** to learn?" and "What have you **Learned**?" Students use the charts as reading comprehension tools. By the end of this lesson, we will discuss how to read long passages using K-W-L charts. The questions will mimic real reading comprehension exams.

Before we begin, here are some tips when reading long passages:

- Take your time when reading.
- Avoid memorizing.
- Avoid skimming through the text.
- The answers are in the passages.
- Avoid getting bogged down by unfamiliar words.

- If you can make notes, do so.
- Look through the questions first.
- Reread the opening and closing paragraphs.
- Identify the keywords or phrases.

Take a look at a couple of passages.

EXERCISE 1

This excerpt is from "Cuban Immigration After the Revolution, 1959-1973" by Franky Abbott.

1. Fill in the two sections of the K-W-L chart below:

WHAT DO I KNOW ABOUT THIS TOPIC?	WHAT DO I WANT TO LEARN ABOUT THIS TOPIC?

The Cuban Revolution occurred **during the Cold War**—a period of post-World War II tension between the Eastern Bloc, led by the communist Soviet Union, and the Western Bloc, led by the democratic United States. Responding to Fidel Castro's Cuba as a communist threat close to home, the US government offered Cuban exiles asylum, financial support, and pathways to permanent residency. **The Cuban Refugee Program was created by President Dwight Eisenhower** in 1960 and expanded by President John F. Kennedy through the "Migration and Refugee Assistance Act" in 1962. It provided financial assistance, health care, educational loans, resettlement, and care of unaccompanied children for the 1,500-2,000 Cubans arriving weekly. **The United States also supported Cuban exodus programs**: Operation Pedro Pan (1960-1962), which brought 14,000 unaccompanied children, and the Freedom Flights (1965-1973), during which the US negotiated with the Cuban government to allow relatives of Cuban refugees to relocate. In 1966, the Cuban Adjustment Act allowed Cuban refugees who came after the Revolution and had lived in the United States for two years to pursue permanent resident status.

2. PART A

What do you think this passage is about?

    a. **It discusses the Cuban revolution and how the US gave their support.**
    b. It discusses the effects of the Cold War.
    c. It discusses the negative effects of the Cuban Adjustment Act.
    d. It describes how the US was a soviet country.

The most suitable answer is "a". The passage talks about the many ways that the US supported the Cubans.

PART B

Which sentence from the passage supports the answer to PART A?

a. In 1966, the Cuban Adjustment Act allowed Cuban refugees who came after the revolution and had lived in the United States for two years to pursue permanent resident status.

b. It provided financial assistance, health care, educational loans, resettlement, and care of unaccompanied children for the 1,500-2,000 Cubans arriving weekly.

c. Responding to Castro's Cuba as a communist threat close to home, the US government offered Cuban exiles asylum, financial support, and pathways to permanent residency.

d. The United States also supported Cuban exodus programs: Operation Pedro Pan (1960-1962)…to allow relatives of Cuban refugees to relocate.

The most suitable answer is c. It summarizes the main idea of the passage.

3. PART A

Who created the Cuban Refugee Program?

a. The Soviet Union
b. Fidel Castro
c. President Dwight Eisenhower
d. President John F. Kennedy

PART B

What act by President John F. Kennedy expanded the program?

a. The Cuban Adjustment Act
b. The Migration and Refugee Assistance Act
c. The Cuban Assistance Act
d. The Migration Adjustment Act

4. In your own words, what happened in 1962?

_____

_____

5. Fill in the last section of the K-W-L chart below.

WHAT HAVE I LEARNED ABOUT THE TOPIC?

EXAMPLE

Read the following dialogue from "Ion" by Plato.

SOCRATES: Welcome, Ion. Are you from your native city of Ephesus?

ION: No, Socrates; but from Epidaurus, where I attended the festival of Asclepius.

SOCRATES: And do the Epidaurians have contests of rhapsodes at the festival?

ION: O yes: and of all sorts of musical performers.

SOCRATES: And were you one of the competitors—and did you succeed?

ION: I obtained the first prize of all, Socrates.

SOCRATES: Well done; and I hope that you will do the same for us at the Panathenaea.

ION: And I will, please heaven.

SOCRATES: I often envy the profession of a rhapsode, Ion: for you have always to wear fine clothes, and to look as beautiful as you can is a part of your art. Then, again, you are obliged to be continually in the company of many good poets: and especially of Homer, who is the best and most divine of them: and to understand him, and not merely learn his words by rote, is a thing greatly to be envied. And no man can be a rhapsode who does not understand the meaning of the poet. For the rhapsode ought to interpret the mind of the poet to his hearers, but how can he interpret him well unless he knows what he means? All this is greatly to be envied.

ION: Very true, Socrates: interpretation has certainly been the most laborious part of my art: and I believe myself able to speak about Homer better than any man: and that neither Metrodorus of Lampsacus, nor Stesimbrotus of Thasos, nor Glaucon, nor anyone else who ever was, had as good ideas about Homer as I have, or as many.

SOCRATES: I am glad to hear you say so, Ion: I see that you will not refuse to acquaint me with them.

ION: Certainly, Socrates: and you really ought to hear how exquisitely I render Homer. I think that the Homeridae should give me a golden crown.

1. PART A

   What do you think this passage is about?

   a. They are comparing each other's professions.

   b. They are insulting each other.

   c. They are declaring their love to each other.

   d. They are declaring their love for art.

The most suitable answer is d. These two characters talk about art in general terms. Both poetry and music are included under the banner of art.

PART B

Which sentence from the passage supports the answer for PART A?

a. O yes; and of all sorts of musical performers.

b. I am glad to hear you say so, Ion: I see that you will not refuse to acquaint me with them.

c. Certainly, Socrates: and you really ought to hear how exquisitely I render Homer. I think that the Homeridae should give me a golden crown.

d. And I will, please heaven.

The most suitable answer is b. This sentence is a response to Ion's declaration for the arts as well. Socrates welcomes him to join him the next time he travels for an arts-related performance.

EXERCISE 2

Read the following excerpt from *Frankenstein: Or, The Modern Prometheus* by Mary Wollstonecraft Shelley (1823).

> *My affection for my guest increases every day. He excites at once my admiration and my pity to an astonishing degree. How can I see so noble a creature destroyed by misery without feeling the most poignant grief? He is so gentle, yet so wise: his mind is so cultivated, and when he speaks, although his words are culled with the choicest art, yet they flow with rapidity and unparalleled eloquence. He is now much recovered from his illness and is continually on the deck, apparently watching for the sledge that preceded his own. Yet, although unhappy, he is not so utterly occupied by his own misery but that he interests himself deeply in the projects of others. He has frequently conversed with me on mine, which I have communicated to him without disguise. He entered attentively into all my arguments in favor of my eventual success and into every minute detail of the measures I had taken to secure it. I was easily led by the sympathy which he evinced to use the language of my heart, to give utterance to the burning ardor of my soul and to say, with all the fervor that warmed me, how gladly I would sacrifice my fortune, my existence, my every hope, to the furtherance of my enterprise. One man's life or death were but a small price to pay for the acquirement of the knowledge which I sought, for the dominion I should acquire and transmit over the elemental foes of our race. As I spoke, a dark gloom spread over my listener's countenance.*

1. PART A

What do you think this passage is about?

a.	The main character despises her guest.	c.	The guest is stand-offish.
b.	**The main character is falling in love.**	d.	The guest despises the main character.

The most suitable answer is b. The passage talks about the main character's growing affection toward the guest. You can understand that the guest's actions and the way the writer speaks about them are pointing towards a love that is blossoming. However, it is hard to say whether the guest feels the same way.

PART B

Which sentence from the passage supports the answer to PART A?

a. One man's life or death were but a small price to pay for the acquirement of the knowledge which I sought, for the dominion I should acquire and transmit over the elemental foes of our race.

b. I was easily led by the sympathy which he evinced to use the language of my heart, to give utterance to the burning ardor of my soul and to say, with all the fervor that warmed me, how gladly I would sacrifice my fortune, my existence, my every hope, to the furtherance of my enterprise.

c. He is so gentle, yet so wise: his mind is so cultivated, and when he speaks, although his words are culled with the choicest art, yet they flow with rapidity and unparalleled eloquence.

d. He has frequently conversed with me on mine, which I have communicated to him without disguise.

The most suitable answer is b. This sentence captures the main idea of the passage, which is located in the middle of the passage.

2. PART A

There are two words that may be unfamiliar to you in the following sentence from the passage. What do they mean?

> *As I spoke, a dark **gloom** spread over my listener's **countenance**.*

i. **Gloom:** _____

ii. **Countenance:** _____

PART B
Rewrite the sentence without using the unfamiliar words.

_____

PRACTICE EXERCISE

Read this passage from *A Tale of Two Cities: A Story of the French Revolution* by Charles Dickens (1859).

Mr. Stryver shouldered his way through the law, like some great engine forcing itself through turbid water, and dragged his useful friend in his wake, like a boat towed astern. As the boat so favored is usually in a rough plight, and mostly under water, so, Sydney had a swamped life of it. But, easy and strong custom, <u>unhappily</u> so much easier and stronger in him than any stimulating sense of desert or disgrace, made it the life he was to lead: and he no more thought of emerging from his state of lion's jackal, than any real jackal may be supposed to think of rising to be a lion. Stryver was rich: had married a florid widow with property and three boys, who had nothing particularly shining about them but the straight hair of their dumpling heads. These three young gentlemen, Mr. Stryver, exuding patronage of the most offensive quality from every pore, had walked before him like three sheep to the quiet corner in Soho, and had offered as pupils to Lucie's husband: delicately saying "Halloa! here are three lumps of bread-and-cheese towards your matrimonial picnic, Darnay!"

The polite rejection of the three lumps of bread-and-cheese had quite bloated Mr. Stryver with indignation, which he afterwards turned to account in the training of the young gentlemen, by directing them to beware of the pride of Beggars, like that tutor-fellow. He was also in the habit of declaiming to Mrs. Stryver, over his full-bodied wine, on the arts Mrs. Darnay had once put in practice to "catch" him, and on the diamond-cut-diamond arts in himself, madam, which had rendered him "not to be caught." Some of his King's Bench familiars, who were occasionally parties to the full-bodied wine and the lie, excused him for the latter by saying that he had told it so often, that he believed it himself—which is surely such an <u>incorrigible aggravation</u> of an originally bad offence, as to justify any such offender's being carried off to some suitably retired spot, and there hanged out of the way.

1. Break down the following words by separating the noun from the prefix/suffix.
    a. Unhappily:_____
    b. Incorrigible: _____
    c. Indignation: _____
    d. Occasionally: _____
2. PART A
    What do you think this passage is about?_____

    _____

    PART B
    Provide three examples as your evidence.

    _____
    _____
    _____

3. What do the similes in this sentence from the passage mean?

    *Mr. Stryver shouldered his way through the law, **like some great engine forcing itself through turbid water,** and dragged his useful friend in his wake, **like a boat towed astern.***

    a. *"like some great engine forcing itself through turbid water"*

    _____
    _____

    b. *"like a boat towed astern"*

    _____
    _____

4. PART A

    Was Mrs. Stryver rich when Mr. Stryver married her?

    _____

    _____

PART B

Give evidence to support your answer.

_____

_____

_____

5. PART A

    Does Mr. Stryver like to drink wine?

    _____

    _____

PART B

Support your answer.

_____

_____

REFLECTION ON LEARNING

Answer the following reflection questions, and feel free to discuss your responses with your teacher or classmate.

- What reading idea or strategy did you learn from this section?

- What new concepts did you learn?

- What methods did you work on in this section?

- What aspect of this section is still not 100 percent clear for you?

- What do you want your teacher to know?

LESSON 9

MAKING INFERENCES AND PREDICTIONS

When reading, you may come across texts that are hard to comprehend. In such cases, you need to "read between the lines" to understand the text's context. To read between the lines means to guess the meaning or information the author does not share explicitly. As the reader, you should develop skills in making inferences or predictions based on what the author says in the text. This lesson will look at <u>identifying character traits</u>, understanding <u>direct/indirect characterization</u>, <u>making conclusions</u>, <u>making inferences</u> and recognizing <u>character descriptions.</u>

Identifying Character Traits

Well-developed characters are like people: they have traits, opinions and motivations. Characterizations are the methods by which storytellers reveal the traits of characters. The first thing you need to do is identify character traits to understand their actions in a story. Take a look at some examples:

> *Cassie is Jake's older sister. One day, they walked home from school. The temperature outside had dropped by 20 degrees. Cassie had carried an extra hoody just in case it became colder. When she looked at Jake, she saw that he was shivering. She offered him the extra hoody. After a few minutes, Jake was smiling.*

From the above example, you can understand that Cassie is kind and considerate because she offered her brother the extra hoody she had. Her action—offering the hoody—led to a positive result: Jake became warm and happy.

> *Bob grabbed a shirt off the floor, sniffed it and flung it back on the same spot. He was looking for a clean shirt to wear but couldn't find any. After a while of rummaging through his room, picking up old pizza boxes and tiptoeing around unwashed plates, he gave up and picked up the same shirt and wore it.*

From the above example, you can understand that Bob is messy and lazy. Instead of doing some laundry, he opts to wear an unwashed shirt.

> *For Frank he had quite an extraordinary affection, though he would not have expressed it so, to himself, for all the world, and a very real admiration of a quite indefinable kind. It was impossible to say why he admired him. Frank did nothing very well, but everything rather well: he played Rugby football, just not well enough to represent his college: he had been in the Lower Boats at Eton, and the Lent Boat of his first year at Cambridge: then he had given up rowing and played lawn-tennis in the summer and fives in the Lent Term just well enough to make a brisk and interesting game. He was not at all learned: he had reached the First Hundred at Eton, and had read Law at Cambridge—that convenient branch of study which for the most part fills the vacuum for intelligent persons who have no particular bent and are heartily sick of classics: and he had taken a Third Class and his degree a day or two before.*
> _____
> *Excerpt from* None Other Gods *by Robert Hugh Benson (1910).*

From the above example, you can understand that Frank is a jack of all trades. Looking at the words in bold, you can tell he has dabbled in many skills rather than gaining expertise by focusing on one.

EXERCISE 1

Read the following excerpt from *Dracula* by Bram Stoker (1897).

> *Then, for the first time in my life, I saw Van Helsing break down. He raised his hands over his head in a sort of mute despair, and then beat his palms together in a helpless way: finally he sat down on a chair, and putting his hands before his face, began to sob, with loud, dry sobs that seemed to come from the very racking of his heart. Then he raised his arms again, as though appealing to the whole universe. "God! God! God!" he said. "What have we done, what has this poor thing done, that we are so sore beset? Is there fate amongst us still, sent down from the pagan world of old, that such things must be, and in such way? This poor mother, all unknowing, and all for the best as she thinks, does such thing as lose her daughter body and soul: and we must not tell her, we must not even warn her, or she die, and then both die. Oh, how we are beset! How are all the powers of the devils against us!" Suddenly he jumped to his feet. "Come," he said, "come, we must see and act. Devils or no devils, or all the devils at once, it matters not: we fight him all the same." He went to the hall-door for his bag: and together we went up to Lucy's room.*

Write down two character traits Van Helsing displays in this excerpt. Give evidence to support your answer.

_____

_____

Understanding Direct/Indirect Characterization

When a writer uses direct characterization, they include direct statements that show the character's personality and traits. When they use indirect characterization, the information is found in the character's thoughts, actions, words and other characters' reactions.

Here are some examples:

Direct: Fatima is so rich, she could buy this house right now.
Indirect: Fatima drove the latest Lamborghini as she headed to her new mansion.

Direct: I was having fun at my sister's wedding.
Indirect: When I checked, it was 4 in the morning. I couldn't believe it. Time had flown by as I joyfully danced with my sister at her wedding.

Direct: Candace is a social butterfly.
Indirect: Candace loves parties. At parties, everyone flocks around her whenever she enters the room.

Direct: He was very smart.
Indirect: After four years at college, he graduated *sum cum laude* from his engineering program.

EXERCISE 2

Rewrite the following sentences.

1. Direct: Freddy is tall.
   Indirect: _____

2. Indirect: I had to look at my phone three times to understand what the text meant.
   Direct: _____

3. Indirect: Talia ran the marathon. Though she was tired halfway through, she continued running.
   Direct: _____

Making Conclusions and Predictions

When we read a text, the writer does not always tell us everything. They may leave out details on purpose. They may also depend on the reader's general knowledge to fill in the blanks. Let's look at several examples:

1. *I lit a candle when the room became darker. I preferred candlelight to electricity, as it was easier on the eyes. Looking at my phone, I sighed. I still had a lot of work to do but I could feel my eyes getting droopy. I wished I had more time to accomplish everything I had set out to do.*

Based on the text, you can understand that this scene is occurring at night. The text tells us the character lights a candle, and her eyes are getting tired. You can infer that the character wishes she had more time during the day to get things done. You can also infer that this text occurs in modern times since the character had the option of using electricity to illuminate her room.

2. *Before heading for her AM shift, Checkers ran three miles with Vivi beside her. Vivi was her best friend, and they were always together since Checkers got him as a pup two years ago. As they approached the house, Vivi ran ahead. Checkers watched as her best friend left her behind.*

Based on the text, you can understand that this scene is happening in the morning because the character is running before her AM shift. You know Vivi is a male dog because the narrator explains that Checkers "got him as a pup." Checkers is a female human because the narrator states that Vivi is "*her* best friend."

Note: In some cases, the text can leave you wondering how the story ends. This is known as a cliffhanger, and fiction writers use this technique all the time. You can make predictions on how the story ends. Let's look at a couple of examples:

3. *Jenny loves to shop for makeup because it makes her happy. For her birthday, she received many gift cards and cash from her family and friends.*

Here, you can predict that Jenny would use the gift cards and cash to shop for more makeup.

4. *Abdul laid out all of his camping gear the night before, so he could pack it all up in the morning. Winnie was beside herself with anticipation as she ran into the house through the doggy trap door. Abdul saw that her feet were dirty, and she left behind muddy footsteps. He tried to put a collar on her, but Winnie was dancing around in excitement.*

Here, you can predict that Abdul was not able to put on the collar on Winnie, and she ended up running around the room. Winnie might have left muddy footprints on his camping gear, causing Abdul to get upset.

EXERCISE 3

All was now bustle and hubbub in the late quiet schoolroom. The scholars were hurried through their lessons without stopping at trifles: those who were nimble skipped over half with impunity, and those who were tardy had a smart application now and then in the rear, to quicken their speed or help them over a tall word. Books were flung aside without being put away on the shelves, inkstands were overturned, benches thrown down, and the whole school was turned loose an hour before the usual time, bursting forth like a legion of young imps, yelping and racketing about the green in joy at their early emancipation.

Excerpt from The Legend Of Sleepy Hollow *by Washington Irving (1820).*

Write two character traits the scholars are showing. Give evidence to support each trait.

_____

_____

Recognizing Character Descriptions

Recognizing character descriptions and traits in literature is an essential skill that students can develop as part of reading comprehension. Understanding the character's actions and thoughts helps them better understand and appreciate the story. Let's take a look at a couple of examples:

*He had to keep still long after she went to bed, for she kept making broken-hearted ejaculations from time to time, tossing unrestfully, and turning over. But at last she was still, only moaning a little in her sleep. Now the boy stole out, **rose gradually by the bedside**, shaded the candlelight with his hand, and stood regarding her. His heart was full of pity for her. He took out his sycamore scroll and placed it by the candle. But something occurred to him, and he lingered considering. His face lighted with a happy solution of his thought: he put the bark hastily in his pocket. **Then he bent over and kissed the faded lips, and straightway made his stealthy exit, latching the door behind him.** He threaded his way back to the ferry landing, found nobody at large there, and walked boldly on board the boat, for he knew she was tenantless except that there was a watchman, who always turned in and slept like a graven image. He untied the skiff at the stern, slipped into it, and was soon **rowing cautiously upstream**. When he had pulled a mile above the village, he started quartering across and bent himself stoutly to his work. He hit the landing on the other side neatly, for this was a familiar bit of work to him. He was moved to capture the skiff, arguing that it might be considered a ship and therefore legitimate prey for a pirate, but he knew a thorough search would be made for it and that might end in revelations. So he stepped ashore and entered the woods.*

Excerpt from The Adventures of Tom Sawyer *by Mark Twain (1876)*

Based on the text, you can infer three traits about the character:

- He is considerate. He got out of bed without wanting to wake the female character.
- He is loving. He kissed the female character before he left.
- He is cautious. He rowed upstream, which can be challenging to do safely.

EXERCISE 4

*"Because it has been all so different with me," Ginger replied. "I never had any one, horse or man, that was kind to me, or that I cared to please, for in the first place I was taken from my mother as soon as I was weaned, and put with a lot of other young colts: none of them cared for me, and I cared for none of them. There was no kind master like yours to look after me, and talk to me, and bring me nice things to eat. **The man that had the care of us never gave me a kind word in my life.** I do not mean that he ill-used me, but he did not care for us one bit further than to see that we had plenty to eat, and shelter in the winter.*

*A footpath ran through our field, and very often **the great boys passing through would fling stones to make us gallop.** I was never hit, but one fine young colt was badly cut in the face, and I should think it would be a scar for life. We did not care for them, but of course **it made us more wild**, and we settled it in our minds that boys were our enemies. We had very good fun in the free meadows, galloping up and down and chasing each other round and round the field: then standing still under the shade of the trees. But when it came to breaking in, that was a bad time for me: several men came to catch me, and when at last they closed me in at one corner of the field, **one caught me by the forelock, another caught me by the nose and held it so tight I could hardly draw my breath:** then another took my under jaw in his hard hand and wrenched my mouth open, and so by force they got on the halter and the bar into my mouth: then one dragged me along by the halter, another flogging behind, and this was the first experience I had of men's kindness: it was all force. They did not give me a chance to know what they wanted. I was high bred and had a great deal of spirit, and was very wild, no doubt, and gave them, I dare say**, plenty of trouble**, but then it was **dreadful to be shut up in a stall day after day instead of having my liberty**, and I fretted and pined and wanted to get loose. You know yourself it's bad enough when you have a kind master and plenty of coaxing, but there was nothing of that sort for me."*

Excerpt from Black Beauty *by Anna Sewell (1877)*

Based on the text, you can infer three character traits Ginger had:

- Ginger was a sad child. She had no freedom and was locked in a stall at all times.
- Ginger is honest. She opens up to the other character about her experiences when she was younger.
- Ginger was rebellious. She mentions how she was a wild horse and gave her caretakers some trouble when she was younger.

Can you list two character traits of the boys and men that Ginger talks about? What is your evidence?

_____

_____

PRACTICE EXERCISE

Read the following excerpt from *Uncle Tom's Cabin* by Harriet Beecher Stowe (1852).

Well, lately Mas'r has been saying that he was a fool to let me marry off the place: that he hates Mr. Shelby and all his tribe, because they are proud, and hold their heads up above him, and that I've got proud notions from you: and he says he won't let me come here anymore, and that I shall take a wife and settle down on his place. At first, he only scolded and grumbled these things: but yesterday he told me that I should take Mina for a wife, and settle down in a cabin with her, or he would sell me down river."

"Why—but you were married to me, by the minister, as much as if you'd been a white man!" said Eliza, simply.

"Don't you know a slave can't be married? There is no law in this country for that: I can't hold you for my wife, if he chooses to part us. That's why I wish I'd never seen you—why I wish I'd never been born: it would have been better for us both,—it would have been better for this poor child if he had never been born. All this may happen to him yet!"

"O, but master is so kind!"

"Yes, but who knows?—he may die—and then he may be sold to nobody knows who. What pleasure is it that he is handsome, and smart, and bright? I tell you, Eliza, that a sword will pierce through your soul for every good and pleasant thing your child is or has: it will make him worth too much for you to keep."

The words **smote** heavily on Eliza's heart: the vision of the trader came before her eyes, and, as if someone had struck her a deadly blow, she turned pale and gasped for breath. She looked nervously out on the **verandah**, where the boy, tired of the grave conversation, had **retired**, and where he was riding triumphantly up and down on Mr. Shelby's walking-stick. She would have spoken to tell her husband her fears, but **checked** herself.

1. Circle the correct meaning of each word in bold, using the context clues from the passage.

i. *"The words **smote** heavily on Eliza's heart."*
   a. struck
   b. carved
   c. leaned
   d. occupied

iii. *"She looked nervously out on the **verandah**."*
   a. forest
   b. field
   c. lake
   d. porch

ii. *"She would have spoken to tell her husband her fears, but **checked** herself."*
   a. stopped
   b. questioned
   c. admired
   d. examined

iv. *"...where the boy, tired of the grave conversation, had **retired**"*
   a. gone to sleep
   b. revolted
   c. withdrew
   d. wild

2. Name one character trait that Eliza's husband (George) displays and explain your reasoning.

_____

_____

3. What does George mean when he says, "a sword will pierce through your soul for every good and pleasant thing your child is or has..."?

_____

_____

4. What do you think will happen after this scene?

_____

_____

Read the following excerpt from President Abraham Lincoln's 1863 Gettysburg Address.

Four score and seven years ago, our fathers brought forth, upon this continent, a new nation, conceived in Liberty, and dedicated to the proposition that all men are created equal. Now we are engaged in a great civil war, testing whether that nation, or any nation, so conceived, and so dedicated, can long endure. We are met here on a great battlefield of that war. We are now have come to dedicate a portion of it as a final resting place of for those who here gave their lives that that nation might live. It is altogether fitting and proper that we should do this. But in a larger sense we cannot dedicate—we can not consecrate—we cannot hallow this ground.

The brave men, living and dead, who struggled here, have consecrated it far above our poor power to add or detract. The world will little note, nor long remember, what we say here, but can never forget what they did here. It is for us, the living, rather to be dedicated here to the unfinished work which they have, thus far, so nobly carried on. It is rather for us to be here dedicated to the great task remaining before us—that from these honored dead we take increased devotion to that cause for which they here gave the last full measure of devotion—that we here highly resolve that these dead shall not have died in vain: that this nation shall have a new birth of freedom: and that this government of the people, by the people, for the people, shall not perish from the earth.

5. If "score" means 20 years, how many years was President Lincoln speaking of when he said, "Four score and seven years ago..."?

_____

_____

6. Name one character trait President Lincoln displays, and explain your reasoning.

_____

_____

7. What does "proposition" mean in the following phrase: "dedicated to the proposition that all men are created equal"?

    a. the constitution   c. the people

    b. the invitation   d. the idea

Read the following excerpt from *Anne of Green Gables* by Lucy Maud Montgomery (1908).

Mr. Phillips's brief reforming energy was over: he didn't want the bother of punishing a dozen pupils: but it was necessary to do something to save his word, so he looked about for a scapegoat and found it in Anne, who had dropped into her seat, gasping for breath, with a forgotten lily wreath hanging askew over one ear and giving her a particularly rakish and disheveled appearance.

"Anne Shirley, since you seem to be so fond of the boys' company we shall indulge your taste for it this afternoon," he said sarcastically. "Take those flowers out of your hair and sit with Gilbert Blythe."

The other boys snickered. Diana, turning pale with pity, plucked the wreath from Anne's hair and squeezed her hand. Anne stared at the master as if turned to stone.
"Did you hear what I said, Anne?" queried Mr. Phillips sternly.
"Yes, sir," said Anne slowly "but I didn't suppose you really meant it."

> *"I assure you I did"—still with the sarcastic inflection which all the children, and Anne especially, hated. It flicked on the raw. "Obey me at once."*
>
> *For a moment, Anne looked as if she meant to disobey. Then, realizing that there was no help for it, she rose haughtily, stepped across the aisle, sat down beside Gilbert Blythe, and buried her face in her arms on the desk. Ruby Gillis, who got a glimpse of it as it went down, told the others going home from school that she'd "actually never seen anything like it—it was so white, with awful little red spots in it."*

8. What character trait does Mr. Phillips display by only punishing Anne? Briefly explain your answer.

_____

9. **PART A**

What type of figurative language is "Anne stared at the master as if turned to stone"?

a. Symbolism
b. Simile

c. Hyperbole
d. Metaphor

PART B

What does the writer mean in this sentence?

a. Anne can't believe that Mr. Phillips is punishing only her.
b. Anne thinks Mr. Phillips has turned to stone.

c. Anne can't believe that Gilbert is punishing her.
d. Anne is relieved that Mr. Phillips' punishment is not worse.

10. What character trait does Anne display in this except? Briefly explain your answer.

_____

_____

11. What do you think happened after this scene? Discuss your answer with a classmate.

_____

_____

Read the following excerpt from *Little Women* by Louisa May Alcott (1869).

> *Charcoal portraits came next, and the entire family hung in a row, looking as wild and **crocky** as if just evoked from a coalbin. Softened into crayon sketches, they did better, for the likenesses were good, and Amy's hair, Jo's nose, Meg's mouth, and Laurie's eyes were pronounced 'wonderfully fine'. A return to clay and plaster followed, and ghostly casts of her acquaintances haunted corners of the house, or tumbled off closet shelves onto people's heads. Children were enticed in as models, till their incoherent accounts of her mysterious doings caused Miss Amy to be regarded in the light of a young ogress. Her efforts in this line, however, were brought to an abrupt close by an untoward accident, which quenched her ardor. Other models failing her for a time, she undertook to cast her own pretty foot, and the family were one day alarmed by an unearthly bumping and screaming and running to the rescue, found the young enthusiast hopping wildly about the shed with her foot held fast in a pan full of plaster, which had hardened with unexpected rapidity. With much difficulty and some danger she was dug out, for Jo was so overcome with laughter while she excavated that her knife went too far, cut the poor foot, and left a lasting memorial of one artistic attempt, at least.*
>
> *After this, Amy subsided, till a mania for sketching from nature set her to haunting river, field, and wood, for picturesque studies, and sighing for ruins to copy. She caught endless colds sitting on damp grass to book 'a delicious bit', composed of a stone, a stump, one mushroom, and a broken mullein stalk, or 'a heavenly mass of clouds', that looked like a choice display of featherbeds when done. She sacrificed her complexion floating on the river in the midsummer sun to study light and shade, and got a wrinkle over her nose trying after 'points of sight', or whatever the squint-and-string performance is called. If 'genius is eternal patience', as Michelangelo affirms, Amy had some claim to the divine attribute, for she persevered in spite of all obstacles, failures, and discouragements, firmly believing that in time she should do something worthy to be called 'high art'.*

12. Write down three character traits Amy displays in this passage and give your evidence for them.

_____

_____

_____

13. What do you think **crocky** means in the phrase "looking as wild and **crocky** as if just evoked from a coalbin"?

a. dirty

b. clean

c. misshapen

d. straight

14. **PART A**

What was Jo's mood when she accidentally cut Amy's foot?

a. Happy

b. Sad

c. Angry

d. Sullen

PART B

Which of the following sentences from the passage supports your answer in PART A?

a. Charcoal portraits came next, and the entire family hung in a row, looking as wild and crocky as if just evoked from a coalbin.

b. She caught endless colds sitting on damp grass to book 'a delicious bit', composed of a stone, a stump, one mushroom, and a broken mullein stalk, or 'a heavenly mass of clouds', that looked like a choice display of featherbeds when done.

c. With much difficulty and some danger she was dug out, for Jo was so overcome with laughter while she excavated that her knife went too far, cut the poor foot, and left a lasting memorial of one artistic attempt, at least.

d. Children were enticed in as models, till their incoherent accounts of her mysterious doings caused Miss Amy to be regarded in the light of a young ogress.

15. **PART A**

What type of figurative language has been used in this sentence?

> *She sacrificed her complexion floating on the river in the midsummer sun to study light and shade.*

a. Symbolism

b. Hyperbole

c. Simile

d. Metaphor

PART B

What did the writer mean in the sentence?

a. Amy sacrificed her life to study.

b. Amy risked getting some shades darker due to the sun's rays.

c. Amy risked losing her skin.

d. Amy sacrificed her love for art.

REFLECTION ON LEARNING

Answer the following reflection questions, and feel free to discuss your responses with your teacher or classmate.

- What reading idea or strategy did you learn from this section?

- What new concepts did you learn?

- What methods did you work on in this section?

- What aspect of this section is still not 100 percent clear for you?

- What do you want your teacher to know?

LESSON 10

USING IMAGERY

Writers use imagery to send messages that connect with readers' physical senses. Imagery can take the form of descriptive and figurative language that helps readers visualize and feel what is happening in their writing. This lesson will discuss the general use of imagery in <u>song lyrics</u>, <u>poems</u> and <u>non-fiction texts</u>.

Imagery can evoke all our senses, either all at once or one at a time. These senses can be visual, auditory (hearing), olfactory (smell), tactile (touch) or gustatory (taste). Take a look at a few examples.

1. It was **dark and dim** in the factory when the police raided it.
   The sense being evoked here is visual through the words "dark and "dim."

2. Leila and Craig were **shouting and screaming** at each other as they ran home.
   The sense being evoked here is auditory through the words "shouting" and "screaming."

3. The juicy and fresh apple is very **sweet and cold**.
   The sense being evoked here is gustatory through the words "sweet" and "cold."

4. As he walked into his local café, Trevor **whiffed** the **aroma** of freshly brewed coffee.
   The sense being evoked here is olfactory through the words "whiff" and "aroma."

5. Gabriela ran her hands over the **soft**, silky dress.
   The sense being evoked here is tactile through the use of the word "soft."

6. The **distant sounds** of drums and **chanting** caught my attention.
   The sense being evoked here is auditory through the use of "distant sounds" and "chanting."

7. Diana was angry and stormed out of the house without a sweater. She is now cold and **shivering** on the patio.
   The sense being evoked is visual through the use of the word "shivering." The sense being evoked is also tactile through the use of the word "cold."

8. Lisa looked at her burger, which was **aromatic** with spices. Her mouth watered in anticipation.
   The sense being evoked here is olfactory through the use of the word "aromatic."

9. My mother **placed the back of her hand on my forehead** to check if I was warm. She suspected I had a fever.

The sense being evoked here is tactile through the use of the character's use of her hand.

> *"Brookfield he had liked, almost from the beginning. He remembered that day of his preliminary interview—**sunny June, with the air full of flower scents and the plick-plock of cricket on the pitch**. Brookfield was playing Barnhurst, and one of the Barnhurst boys, a chubby little fellow, made a brilliant century. Queer that a thing like that should stay in the memory so clearly."*
>
> *Excerpt from* Goodbye, Mr. Chips *by James Hilton (1938)*

This excerpt uses three senses. The writer uses the word **sunny** to refer to visual imagery. **Flower scents** evoke a sense of smell and **plick-plock** refers to the sense of hearing.

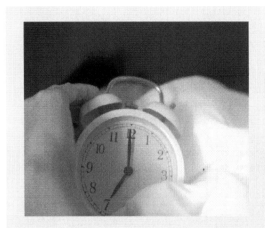

*It was a rimy morning, and very **damp**. I had seen the damp lying on the outside of my little window, as if some goblin had been crying there all night, and using the window for a pocket-handkerchief. Now, I saw the **damp** lying on the bare hedges and spare grass, like a coarser sort of spiders' webs: hanging itself from twig to twig and blade to blade. On every rail and gate, **wet lay clammy**, and the **marsh mist was so thick**, that the wooden finger on the post directing people to our village—a direction which they never accepted, for they never came there—was invisible to me until I was quite close under it.*

Excerpt from Great Expectations *by Charles Dickens (1861).*

In this excerpt, the repeated use of the words **damp** and **wet** makes us feel how miserable it was for the character to be that damp on a cold morning. Additionally, the **thick marsh mist** helps us visualize the scene of the morning in the marshland.

EXERCISE 1

The fans traveled across the country to watch the baseball game. They were tired, dusty and thirsty but excited to hear the sound of the bats hitting the ball. Even the creaky and splintery benches on which they had to sit did not dampen their mood. With empty bellies and parched throats, they cheered their team on.

Name at least two senses the writer has evoked and the words used to do so.

_____

_____

Imagery in Song Lyrics

Imagery is used in lyrics to clarify and deepen the meaning of songs. Singers and songwriters do this to increase the listener's emotions and make the song memorable.

Let's take a look at three examples:

SONG/SINGER	LYRICS	MEANING
"So In Love" by Cole Porter (1948)	*Strange, dear, but true, dear,* *When I'm close to you dear,* *The stars fill the sky,* *So in love with you am I.*	3. The writer uses a metaphor in the third line. This is an exaggeration but shows how the singer feels when he is close to the person he loves. 4. The word "dear" has been used to offer a feeling of tenderness and warmth.
"Happy" by Pharrell William (2013)	*I'm a hot air balloon that could go to space* *With the air, like I don't care baby by the way* *Huh, because I'm happy* *Clap along if you feel like a room without a roof...* *Here come bad news, talking this and that...*	5. The writer uses a simile in *"clap along if you feel like a room without a roof"* to compare a person to a room without a roof. A room without a roof is also a metaphor for freedom since this type of room has no limits. 6. The writer also uses a metaphor in the line, *"I'm a hot air balloon that can go to space."* This has been used to express happiness that makes someone feel they are at a great height with no constrictions.
"Diamond" by Rihanna (2012)	*Shine bright like a diamond* *Shine bright like a diamond* *Find light in the beautiful sea, I choose to be happy* *You and I, you and I, we're like diamonds in the sky* *You're a shooting star I see, a vision of ecstasy* *When you hold me, I'm alive...*	7. There is a simile in the first line. The writer compares a person's character trait ("shining bright") to a sparkling diamond. 8. The phrase *"You're a shooting star I see"* is a metaphor. A person is compared to a shooting star without using *like* or *as*.

EXERCISE 2

Make me your radio
Turn me up when you feel low
The melody was meant for you
Just sing along to my stereo...
If it was an old-school fifty pound boombox.

"Stereo Hearts" by Gym Class Heroes (2011)

- What type of figurative language is used in these lyrics? _____

_____

- Summarize what the writer means when they use the figurative language in this way.

Imagery in Poems

Poets are known for applying imagery in their work, mainly to create visual representations in our minds. They take advantage of the fact that we read plain and explicit texts all the time. Often, we read a poem as an escape from regular day-to-day reading. Below are three examples.

TITLE/POET	POEMS	MEANING
"My November Guest" by Robert Frost (1913)	*"My Sorrow, when she's here with me,* *Thinks these **dark days** of autumn rain* *Are beautiful as days can be:* *She loves the **bare**, the **withered** tree:* *She walked the **sodden pasture** lane."*	• In the second line, the poet uses visual imagery in the phrase **dark days**. • The fourth line, "the **bare, withered tree**" is also an example of visual imagery. • In the fifth line, the **sodden pasture** is an instance of tactile imagery.
"Fish" by Elizabeth Bishop (1911)	*his brown skin hung in strips* *like ancient wallpaper,* *and its pattern of darker brown* *was like wallpaper:* *shapes like full-blown roses* *stained and lost through age.*	• This excerpt contains a lot of visual imagery that tells us the state of the fish.
"Summer Night" by Alfred Tennyson (date unknown)	*And like a ghost, she **glimmers** on to me.* *Now lies the Earth all Danaë to the stars,* *And all thy heart lies open unto me.* *Now slides the silent **meteor** on, and leaves* *A **shining** furrow, as thy thoughts in me.* *Now folds the lily all her **sweetness** up,* *And **slips** into the bosom of the lake* *So fold thyself, my dearest, thou, and slip.*	• The words **shining, sweetness, slips** and **glimmers** appeal to our visual senses as the poet creates a beautiful picture of the night. • The shooting star (**meteor**) and its shiny tail is a sparkling image he uses of a young man and woman. • The beautiful atmosphere of twilight and the darkness filled with stars are examples of visual imagery.

EXERCISE 3

The whiskey on your breath,
Could make a small boy dizzy:
But I hung on like death:
Such waltzing was not easy.
We romped until the pans,
Slid from the kitchen shelf:
My mother's countenance,
Could not unfrown itself

"My Papa's Waltz" by Theodore Roethke (1942)

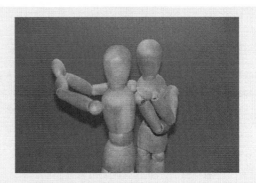

Summarize what you think the poet means in this poem.

_____

_____

PRACTICE EXERCISE

Read the following excerpt from *Moby-Dick Or, The Whale* by Herman Melville (1851).

> At length as the craft was cast to one side, and ran ranging along with the White Whale's flank, he seemed strangely oblivious of its advance—as the whale sometimes will—and Ahab was fairly within the smoky mountain mist, which, thrown off from the whale's spout, curled round his great, Monadnock hump: he was even thus close to him: when, with body arched back, and both arms lengthwise high-lifted to the poise, he darted his fierce iron, and his far fiercer curse into the hated whale. As both steel and curse sank to the socket, as if sucked into a morass, Moby Dick sideways writhed: spasmodically rolled his nigh flank against the bow, and, without staving a hole in it, so suddenly canted the boat over, that had it not been for the elevated part of the gunwale to which he then clung, Ahab would once more have been tossed into the sea.
>
> As it was, three of the oarsmen—who foreknew not the precise instant of the dart, and were therefore unprepared for its effects—these were flung out: but so fell, that, in an instant two of them clutched the gunwale again, and rising to its level on a combing wave, hurled themselves bodily inboard again: the third man helplessly dropping astern, but still afloat and swimming. Almost simultaneously, with a mighty volition of ungraduated, instantaneous swiftness, the White Whale darted through the weltering sea. But when Ahab cried out to the steersman to take new turns with the line, and hold it so: and commanded the crew to turn round on their seats, and tow the boat up to the mark: the moment the treacherous line felt that double strain and tug, it snapped in the empty air!
>
> "What breaks in me? Some sinew cracks!—'tis whole again: oars! oars! Burst in upon him!"

1. What is this passage about? Discuss your answer with a classmate.

_____

_____

2. **PART A**
What happened when Ahab shot at Moby Dick?

   a. Ahab jumped up in joy.
   b. Moby Dick flipped the boat over.
   c. Ahab and Moby Dick made a truce.
   d. Moby Dick killed Ahab.

   PART B
   Which sentence from the passage supports your answer to Part A?

   a. Moby Dick sideways writhed: spasmodically rolled his nigh flank against the bow, and, without staving a hole in it, so suddenly canted the boat over….
   b. At length as the craft was cast to one side, and ran ranging along with the White Whale's flank, he seemed strangely oblivious of its advance…
   c. Ahab would once more have been tossed into the sea….
   d. …but so fell, that, in an instant two of them clutched the gunwale again….

3. **PART A**

What sense is being evoked in this sentence from the passage?

Almost simultaneously, with a mighty volition of ungraduated, instantaneous swiftness, the White Whale darted through the weltering sea.

a. Olfactory

b. Gustatory

c. Visual

d. Tactile

PART B

Which of the following words from the passage supports your answer in PART A?

a. simultaneously

b. mighty

c. volition

d. instantaneous

4. Can you make a text-to-self connection? Compare your answer with a classmate.

_____

_____

5. In your own words, how do you think this scene ends? Provide evidence for your answer.

_____

_____

Read the following excerpt from the poem "Phantasmagoria and Other Poems: Size and Tears" by Lewis Carroll (1869).

When on the sandy shore I sit,
Beside the salt sea-wave,
And fall into a weeping fit
Because I dare not shave—
A little whisper at my ear
Enquires the reason of my fear.

I answer "If that ruffian Jones
Should recognize me here,
He'd bellow out my name in tones
Offensive to the ear:
He chaffs me so on being stout
(A thing that always puts me out)."

Ah me! I see him on the cliff!
Farewell, farewell to hope,
If he should look this way, and if
He's got his telescope!
To whatsoever place I flee,
My odious rival follows me!

6. What is the theme of the poem?

_____

_____

7. Can you make a text-to-self connection to the text?

_____

_____

8. How has the poet evoked the visual sense?

_____

_____

9. How has the poet evoked the auditory sense?

_____

_____

Read the following lyrics for "I'll Make A Man Out of You" from the movie _Mulan_ (1998).

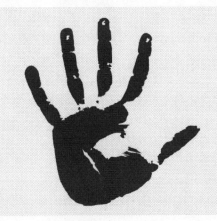

Tranquil as a forest but on fire within
Once you find your center, you are sure to win
You're a spineless, pale, pathetic lot
And you haven't got a clue
Somehow I'll make a man out of you
I'm never gonna catch my breath
Say goodbye to those who knew me
Boy, was I a fool in school for cutting gym
This guy's got 'em scared to death
Hope he doesn't see right through me
Now I really wish that I knew how to swim

10. What is the song's theme? Discuss your answer with a classmate.

_____

11. How has the writer evoked the visual sense? Discuss with a classmate.

_____

_____

REFLECTION ON LEARNING

Answer the following reflection questions, and feel free to discuss your responses with your teacher or classmate.

- What reading idea or strategy did you learn from this section?

- What new concepts did you learn?

- What methods did you work on in this section?

- What aspect of this section is still not 100 percent clear for you?

- What do you want your teacher to know?

LESSON 11

NARRATOR'S POINT OF VIEW

When thinking about the point of view of a person telling a story (the narrator), we should consider the relationship between the narrator and the people (the characters) of the story. This lesson will focus on fiction stories and two types of narration: first-person and third-person.

First-Person Narration

The narrator is usually the protagonist or central character in the story. However, even if this character is not the protagonist, he or she is directly involved in the story's events and tells the tale firsthand. First-person narration is easy to identify because the narrator will use first-person pronouns: I, me, my, our, us, we, myself, *and* ourselves. *Let's take a look at a few examples:*

1. *I don't think I can walk anymore. I'm too tired to move any further.*

2. *Tatiana and I went to the library to catch up on our homework.*

3. *We went, by ourselves, to the courthouse to pay off your parking fines.*

4. *I was too angry to maintain my cool.*

5. *It had rained earlier, and the dampness of the grass made my running shoes damp. But I didn't mind. I was having a good time running to the rhythm of my favorite song playing through my AirPods. I cleared my head and thought of nothing but the music filling my head.*

6. *Traffic had to be blocked off to allow the parade to march down the street. Music filled the air as the leader encouraged the performers to move along. He blew a whistle in time with the rhythm and tempo of the music. The street was lined with people clapping along and laughing, excited about the parade.*

7. *My first impression as I opened the door was that a fire had broken out, for the room was so filled with smoke that the light of the lamp upon the table was blurred by it. As I entered, however, my fears were set at rest, for it was the acrid fumes of strong coarse tobacco which took me by the throat and set me coughing. Through the haze, I had a vague vision of Holmes in his dressing-gown coiled up in an armchair with his black clay pipe between his lips. Several rolls of paper lay around him.*

Excerpt from The Hound of the Baskervilles *by Sir Arthur Conan Doyle (1902).*

EXERCISE 1

The following excerpt is from *Black Beauty* by Anna Sewell (1877).

> *The squire and Farmer Grey had worked together, as they said, for more than twenty years to get check-reins on the cart-horses done away with, and in our parts you seldom saw them: and sometimes, if mistress met a heavily laden horse with his head strained up, she would stop the carriage and get out, and reason with the driver in her sweet serious voice, and try to show him how foolish and cruel it was. I don't think any man could withstand our mistress. I wish all ladies were like her. Our master, too, used to come down very heavy sometimes. I remember he was riding me toward home one morning when we saw a powerful man driving toward us in a light pony chaise, with a beautiful little bay pony, with slender legs and a high-bred sensitive head and face. Just as he came to the park gates the little thing turned toward them: the man, without word or warning, wrenched the creature's head round with such a force and suddenness that he nearly threw it on its haunches. Recovering itself it was going on, when he began to lash it furiously. The pony plunged forward, but the strong, heavy handheld the pretty creature back with force almost enough to break its jaw, while the whip still cut into him. It was a dreadful sight to me, for I knew what fearful pain it gave that delicate little mouth: but master gave me the word, and we were up with him in a second.*

Summarize why this passage is considered a first-person narration. Discuss your answer with a classmate.

_____

_____

Third-Person Narration

With this type of narration, the narrator tells the story of another person or group of people. The narrator may be far removed from or not involved in the story. He or she may be a supporting character supplying narration for a hero. In this type of story, there is the frequent use of *he, she, them, they, him, her, his* and *their*. Below are a few examples:

1. They held their ground and refused to barge. They waited for the doors to open so they could buy the latest PlayStation.

2. Mary was silent. She tried to control her anger because she wanted to avoid a confrontation. The biker was not making it easy as he continued to berate her.

3. The room was dark and gloomy. Chad couldn't find the energy to get up and switch on the lights. He was falling down. He decided to just close his eyes and hope the sadness would fade away.

4. "Roland is responsible for the accounts!" Yolanda shouted in an effort to make her point come across. She felt that the board of directors was looking for a scapegoat for the missing money.

5. Twaila and Frankie took a boat ride on the Nile River. They couldn't believe their luck. They had won a competition to have a holiday in Egypt.

EXERCISE 2

Read the following passage.

The Law of the Jungle lays down very clearly that any wolf may, when he marries, withdraw from the Pack he belongs to. But as soon as his cubs are old enough to stand on their feet, he must bring them to the Pack Council, which is generally held once a month at full moon, in order that the other wolves may identify them. After that inspection the cubs are free to run where they please, and until they have killed their first buck no excuse is accepted if a grown wolf of the Pack kills one of them. The punishment is death where the murderer can be found and if you think for a minute you will see that this must be so.

Excerpt from The Jungle Book by Rudyard Kipling (1894).

Summarize why this passage is considered a third-person narration in your notebook.

Note: In some cases, a text can use both narrative forms, allowing the writer to include more points of view.

PRACTICE EXERCISE

Read the following excerpt from *Little Women* by Louisa May Alcott (1869).

I don't know whether the study of Shakespeare helped her to read character, or the natural instinct of a woman for what was honest, brave, and strong: but while endowing her imaginary heroes with every perfection under the sun, Jo was discovering a live hero, who interested her in spite of many human imperfections. Mr. Bhaer, in one of their conversations, had advised her to study simple, true, and lovely characters, wherever she found them, as good training for a writer. Jo took him at his word, for she coolly turned round and studied him—a proceeding which would have much surprised him, had he known it, for the worthy Professor was very humble in his own conceit. Why everybody liked him was what puzzled Jo, at first. He was neither rich nor great, young nor handsome: in no respect what is called fascinating, imposing, or brilliant: and yet he was as attractive as a genial fire, and people seemed to gather about him as naturally as about a warm hearth. He was poor, yet always appeared to be giving something away: a stranger, yet everyone was his friend: no longer young, but as happy-hearted as a boy: plain and peculiar, yet his face looked beautiful to many, and his oddities were freely forgiven for his sake. Jo often watched him, trying to discover the charm, and, at last, decided that it was benevolence which worked the miracle. If he had any sorrow, "it sat with its head under its wing," and he turned only his sunny side to the world. There were lines upon his forehead, but Time seemed to have touched him gently, remembering how kind he was to others. The pleasant curves about his mouth were the memorials of many friendly words and cheery laughs: his eyes were never cold or hard, and his big hand had a warm, strong grasp that was more expressive than words.

1. What point of view is used in this passage? Discuss your answer with a classmate.

2. Support your answer above with evidence.

Read the following excerpt from *The Legend Of Sleepy Hollow* by Washington Irving (1820).

But if there was a pleasure in all this, while snugly cuddling in the chimney corner of a chamber that was all of a ruddy glow from the crackling wood fire, and where, of course, no specter dared to show its face, it was dearly purchased by the terrors of his subsequent walk homewards. What fearful shapes and shadows beset his path, amidst the dim and ghastly glare of a snowy night! With what wistful look did he eye every trembling ray of light streaming across the waste fields from some distant window! How often was he appalled by some shrub covered with snow, which, like a sheeted specter, beset his very path! How often did he shrink with curdling awe at the sound of his own steps on the frosty crust beneath his feet: and dread to look over his shoulder, lest he should behold some uncouth being tramping close behind him! And how often was he thrown into complete dismay by some rushing blast, howling among the trees, in the idea that it was the Galloping Hessian on one of his nightly scourings!

3. What point of view is used in this passage? Discuss your answer with a classmate.

_____

4. Support your answer above with evidence.

_____

_____

Read the following excerpt from *The Secret Garden* by Frances Hodgson Burnett (1911).

He is now much recovered from his illness and is continually on the deck, apparently watching for the sledge that preceded his own. Yet, although unhappy, he is not so utterly occupied by his own misery but that he interests himself deeply in the projects of others. He has frequently conversed with me on mine, which I have communicated to him without disguise. He entered attentively into all my arguments in favor of my eventual success and into every minute detail of the measures I had taken to secure it. I was easily led by the sympathy which he evinced to use the language of my heart, to give utterance to the burning ardor of my soul and to say, with all the fervor that warmed me, how gladly I would sacrifice my fortune, my existence, my every hope, to the furtherance of my enterprise. One man's life or death were but a small price to pay for the acquirement of the knowledge which I sought, for the dominion I should acquire and transmit over the elemental foes of our race. As I spoke, a dark gloom spread over my listener's countenance. At first I perceived that he tried to suppress his emotion: he placed his hands before his eyes, and my voice quivered and failed me as I beheld tears trickle fast from between his fingers: a groan burst from his heaving breast. I paused: at length he spoke, in broken accents: "Unhappy man! Do you share my madness? Have you drunk also of the intoxicating draught? Hear me: let me reveal my tale, and you will dash the cup from your lips!"

5. What point of view is used in this passage? Discuss with a classmate.

_____

6. Support your answer above with evidence.

_____

_____

Read the following excerpt from *Dracula* by Bram Stoker (1897).

When we started, the crowd round the inn door, which had by this time swelled to a considerable size, all made the sign of the cross and pointed two fingers towards me. With some difficulty, I got a fellow passenger to tell me what they meant: he would not answer at first, but on learning that I was English, he explained that it was a charm or guard against the evil eye. This was not very pleasant for me, just starting for an unknown place to meet an unknown man: but everyone seemed so kind-hearted, and so sorrowful, and so sympathetic that I could not but be touched. I shall never forget the last glimpse which I had of the inn-yard and its crowd of picturesque figures, all crossing themselves, as they stood round the wide archway, with its background of rich foliage of oleander and orange trees in green tubs clustered in the center of the yard. Then our driver, whose wide linen drawers covered the whole front of the box-seat— "gotza" they call them—cracked his big whip over his four small horses, which ran abreast, and we set off on our journey.

7. What point of view is used in this passage?

_____

8. Support your answer above with evidence.

_____

REFLECTION ON LEARNING

Answer the following reflection questions, and feel free to discuss your responses with your teacher or classmate.

- What reading idea or strategy did you learn from this section?

- What new concepts did you learn?

- What methods did you work on in this section?

- What aspect of this section is still not 100 percent clear for you?

- What do you want your teacher to know?

LESSON 12

HOW TO READ VISUAL INFORMATION AND DATA

To interpret and extract data from graphs and charts, you need to understand visual representations. A single image or visual representation can contain a lot of useful information. This lesson will look at interpreting data from tables, graphs, pie charts and bar charts.

The following table shows the prices of different types of printing machinery available in the early 1800s.

	1806.	1811.	1819.	1827.	1831.	1841.	1860.	1866.	1876.	1893.
Pica	$ 0.44	$ 0.55	$ 0.44	$ 0.42	$ 0.36	$ 0.38	$ 0.32	$ 0.56	$ 0.46	$ 0.32
Small Pica	.48	.58	.48	.46	.38	.40	.34	.58	.48	.34
Lg. Primer	.56	.66	.56	.50	.40	.42	.36	.62	.50	.36
Bourgeois	.66	.76	.66	.58	.46	.46	.40	.66	.52	.38
Brevier	.76	.86	.76	.70	.56	.54	.44	.70	.55	.42
Minion	1.03	1.13	1.00	.88	.70	.66	.48	.76	.58	.46
Nonpareil	1.40	1.75	1.40	1.20	.90	.84	.58	.84	.66	.52
Agate				1.44	1.10	1.08	.72	1.00	.76	.60
Pearl				1.75	1.40	1.40	1.08	1.40	1.20	1.20
Diamond							1.60	1.80	1.62	1.60

Sourced from The American Printer: A Manual of Typography *by Thomas MacKellar (1885)*

The horizontal axis (the top row) gives the year, while the vertical axis (the column to your left) indicates the type of machinery that was sold. This table shows the cost of each piece of machinery. Let's take a look at some questions:

1. How much did a Brevier type machine cost in 1860? Your answer would be **$0.44**.
2. How much did a Diamond type machine cost in 1811? Your answer would be **nothing**.
3. Which type of machine was the cheapest to buy in 1893? Your answer would be **Pica.**
4. Which type of machine was the most expensive to buy in 1831? Your answer would be **Pearl.**

EXERCISE 1

5. In which year did Agate type machinery have the lowest cost? Your answer would be _____.
6. Which year did Pica type machinery cost the most? Your answer would be _____.
7. Which type of machinery had the highest cost between 1841 and 1866? Your answer _____.
8. Did Lg. Primer type machinery have the highest cost in 1893? Your answer would be _____.
9. In which year did Bourgeois type machinery cost the cheapest? _____.
10. Which type machinery had the highest cost between 1806 and 1841? _____.
11. In which year did Minion type machinery have the highest cost? _____.
12. Did Nonpareil type machinery show a rise or decline in price? _____.

Reading a Chart

The following bar chart displays student punctuality at a local college. The horizontal axis (the bottom row) indicates the number of students, and the vertical axis (the column to your left) indicates the day of the week.

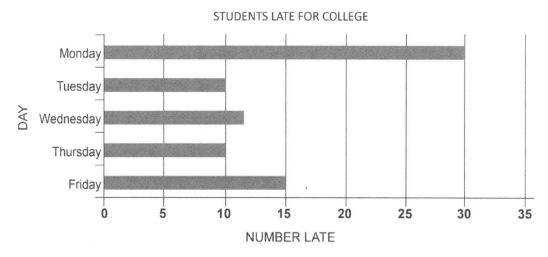

EXERCISE 2
Let's look at some questions based on the chart.

1. On which two days were the same number of students late? _____.

2. How many students were late on Monday? _____.

3. How many more students were late on Friday compared to Tuesday? _____.

4. Using a text-to-world connection, why do you think so many students were late on Monday?

_____

_____

EXERCISE 3
The following is a table showing the results of the 10K women's race at the 2016 Rio Olympics:

RANK	PARTICIPANT	COUNTRY	TIMING
G	Almaz Ayana	Ethiopia	29:17
S	Vivian Jepkemoi Cheruiyot	Kenya	29:32
B	Tirunesh Dibaba	Ethiopia	29:42
4	Alice Aprot Nawowuna	Kenya	29:53
5	Betsy Saina	Kenya	30:07
6	Molly Huddle	USA	30:13
7	Yasemin Can	Turkey	30:26

1. How many were runners from Kenya? Your answer would be **3**.

2. What is the slowest time? Your answer would be_____.

3. What does the letter "S" in Vivian's rank column mean? Your answer_____.

4. What would have happened if Tirunesh had run 11 seconds faster than Vivian? Your answer would be **she would have won the silver medal.**

5. Which country did most winners represent? Your answer would be_____.

6. Using a text-to-self connection, how would you feel if you won a gold medal?

_____

_____

PRACTICE EXERCISES
The following bar chart shows the number of pizzas sold in a day by a business.

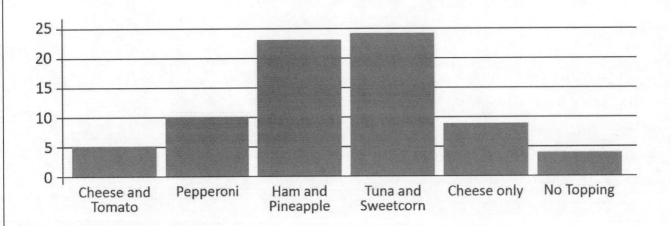

1. Which type of pizza sold the most? _____

2. What type of pizza sold the least? _____

3. How many no-topping pizzas were sold? _____

4. How many cheese-only pizzas were sold? _____

5. What is the difference between the number of pepperoni pizzas sold and the number of tuna-and-

   sweetcorn pizzas sold? _____

6. Using a text-to-self connection, why do you think no-topping pizzas did not sell much?

_____

The following is a climate graph for the District of Columbia.

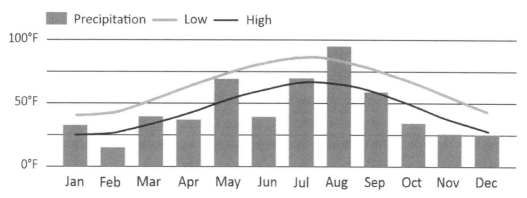

7. Which month was the warmest?_____

8. Which month was the coldest? _____

9. When was the biggest temperature change? _____

10. What was the temperature in June? _____

11. Using a text-to-self connection, what was the weather like in August?

_____

The following table from *Common Sense* by Thomas Paine (1776) shows the costs of guns and ships that the British Navy purchased in 1757.

SHIPS	GUNS	COST OF ONE	COST OF ALL.
		Cost in £ (Pounds sterling)	
6	100	35,553	213,318
12	90	29,886	358,632
12	80	23,638	283,656
43	70	17,785	764,755
35	60	14,197	496,895
40	50	10,606	424,240
45	40	7,558	340,110
58	20	3,710	215,180
85	Sloops, bombs and fireships, one with another, at	2,000	170,000
Cost			3,266,786
Remains for Guns			233,214
			3,500,000

12. **PART A**

Does the overall cost decrease as the number of guns purchased decreases?

_____

PART B

Support your answer.

_____

_____

13. How much was spent when the Navy bought 35 ships?

_____

14. How much was spent when the Navy bought 50 guns?

_____

15. How much did the Navy spend when they did not buy any guns?

_____

REFLECTION ON LEARNING

Answer the following reflection questions, and feel free to discuss your responses with your teacher or classmate.

- What reading idea or strategy did you learn from this section?

- What new concepts did you learn?

- What methods did you work on in this section?

- What aspect of this section is still not 100 percent clear for you?

- What do you want your teacher to know?

LESSON 13

MORE PRACTICE PASSAGES

We are nearing the end of the book. Before we get to the practice test section, use the passages below to practice the reading strategies we have covered in the previous lessons. Use your own words to answer the comprehension questions.

Read the following excerpt from *A Tale Of Two Cities: A Story Of The French Revolution* by Charles Dickens (1859).

Madame Defarge, his wife, sat in the shop behind the counter as he came in. Madame Defarge was a stout woman of about his own age, with a watchful eye that seldom seemed to look at anything, a large hand heavily ringed, a steady face, strong features, and great composure of manner. There was a character about Madame Defarge, from which one might have predicated that she did not often make mistakes against herself in any of the reckonings over which she presided. Madame Defarge being sensitive to cold, was wrapped in fur, and had a quantity of bright shawl twined about her head, though not to the concealment of her large earrings. Her knitting was before her, but she had laid it down to pick her teeth with a toothpick. Thus engaged, with her right elbow supported by her left hand, Madame Defarge said nothing when her lord came in, but coughed just one grain of cough. This, in combination with the lifting of her darkly defined eyebrows over her toothpick by the breadth of a line, suggested to her husband that he would do well to look round the shop among the customers, for any new customer who had dropped in while he stepped over the way.

1. What can you infer from this passage?

   _____

   _____

2. What do you think was Madame Defarge's purpose in this scene?

   _____

   _____

3. Name four character traits that Madame Defarge shows.

   _____

   _____

4. Read the following sentence from the passage.

   *There was a character about Madame Defarge, from which one might have **predicated** that she did not often make mistakes against herself in any of the **reckonings** over which she **presided**.*

Using context clues, what do the following words mean?

   a. predicated:_____

   b. reckonings:_____

   c. presided:_____

5. Transform the following sentences from the passage into a first-person narration.

> *Madame Defarge being sensitive to cold, was wrapped in fur, and had a quantity of bright shawl twined about her head, though not to the concealment of her large earrings. Her knitting was before her, but she had laid it down to pick her teeth with a toothpick.*

_____

_____

_____

Read the following excerpt from *The Adventures of Tom Sawyer* by Mark Twain (1876).

> *ONE of the reasons why Tom's mind had drifted away from its secret troubles was, that it had found a new and weighty matter to interest itself about. Becky Thatcher had stopped coming to school. Tom had struggled with his pride a few days, and tried to "whistle her down the wind," but failed. He began to find himself hanging around her father's house, nights, and feeling very miserable. She was ill. What if she should die! There was distraction in the thought. He no longer took an interest in war, nor even in piracy. The charm of life was gone: there was nothing but dreariness left. He put his hoop away, and his bat: there was no joy in them anymore. His aunt was concerned. She began to try all manner of remedies on him. She was one of those people who are infatuated with patent medicines and all new-fangled methods of producing health or mending it. She was an inveterate experimenter in these things. When something fresh in this line came out she was in a fever, right away, to try it: not on herself, for she was never ailing, but on anybody else that came handy. She was a subscriber for all the "Health" periodicals and phrenological frauds: and the solemn ignorance they were inflated with was breath to her nostrils.*
>
> *All the "rot" they contained about ventilation, and how to go to bed, and how to get up, and what to eat, and what to drink, and how much exercise to take, and what frame of mind to keep one's self in, and what sort of clothing to wear, was all gospel to her, and she never observed that her health-journals of the current month customarily upset everything they had recommended the month before. She was as simple-hearted and honest as the day was long, and so she was an easy victim. She gathered together her quack periodicals and her quack medicines, and thus armed with death, went about on her pale horse, metaphorically speaking, with "hell following after." But she never suspected that she was not an angel of healing and the balm of Gilead in disguise, to the suffering neighbors.*

6. What can you infer from this passage? Discuss your answer with a classmate.

_____

_____

7. Part A- In what did Tom lose interest?

_____

Part B- Why did he lose interest?

_____

_____

8. What did the writer mean in this sentence?

> *When something fresh in this line came out, she was in a fever, right away, to try it: not on herself, for she was never ailing, but on anybody else that came handy.*

_____

_____

9. Can you make a text-to-self connection with the following sentence using the following phrase?

> *ONE of the reasons why Tom's mind had drifted away from its secret troubles was, that it had found a new and weighty matter to interest itself about.*

I've felt like that when _____

_____

Read the following excerpt from *The Velveteen Rabbit* by Margery Williams (1922).

> *That night, and for many nights after, the Velveteen Rabbit slept in the Boy's bed. At first he found it rather uncomfortable, for the Boy hugged him very tight, and sometimes he rolled over on him, and sometimes he pushed him so far under the pillow that the Rabbit could scarcely breathe. And he missed, too, those long moonlight hours in the nursery, when all the house was silent, and his talks with the Skin Horse. But very soon he grew to like it, for the Boy used to talk to him, and made nice tunnels for him under the bedclothes that he said were like the burrows the real rabbits lived in. And they had splendid games together, in whispers, when Nana had gone away to her supper and left the night-light burning on the mantelpiece. And when the Boy dropped off to sleep, the Rabbit would snuggle down close under his little warm chin and dream, with the Boy's hands clasped close round him all night long. And so time went on, and the little Rabbit was very happy—so happy that he never noticed how his beautiful velveteen fur was getting shabbier and shabbier, and his tail becoming unsewn, and all the pink rubbed off his nose where the Boy had kissed him. Spring came, and they had long days in the garden, for wherever the Boy went the Rabbit went too. He had rides in the wheelbarrow, and picnics on the grass, and lovely fairy huts built for him under the raspberry canes behind the flower border. And once, when the Boy was called away suddenly to go out to tea, the Rabbit was left out on the lawn until long after dusk, and Nana had to come and look for him with the candle because the Boy couldn't go to sleep unless he was there. He was wet through with the dew and quite earthy from diving into the burrows the Boy had made for him in the flower bed, and Nana grumbled as she rubbed him off with a corner of her apron.*

10. What can you infer from this passage? Discuss your answer with a classmate.

_____

11. Using the entire text as evidence, can you make a text-to-world connection with the following sentence?

> *Spring came, and they had long days in the garden, for wherever the boy went the Rabbit went too.*

_____

_____

12. What do you think happened after this scene?

_____

_____

13. Read the following sentence from the passage:

> *And when the Boy <u>dropped</u> off to sleep, the Rabbit would snuggle down close under his little warm chin and dream, with the Boy's hands <u>clasped</u> close round him all night long.*

Using context clues, write words similar to the following:

a. dropped: _____

b. clasped: _____

14. What does this sentence tell you about the character from whose point of view we are reading the text? Support your answer with evidence.

> *But very soon he grew to like it, for the Boy used to talk to him, and made nice tunnels for him under the bedclothes that he said were like the burrows the real rabbits lived in.*

Read the following excerpt from *The Adventures of Sherlock Holmes* by Arthur Conan Doyle (1876).

"The ceremony, which was performed at St. George's, Hanover Square, was a very quiet one, no one being present save the father of the bride, Mr. Aloysius Doran, the Duchess of Balmoral, Lord Backwater, Lord Eustace and Lady Clara St. Simon (the younger brother and sister of the bridegroom), and Lady Alicia Whittington. The whole party proceeded afterwards to the house of Mr. Aloysius Doran, at Lancaster Gate, where breakfast had been prepared. It appears that some little trouble was caused by a woman, whose name has not been ascertained, who endeavored to force her way into the house after the bridal party, alleging that she had some claim upon Lord St. Simon. It was only after a painful and prolonged scene that she was ejected by the butler and the footman.

The bride, who had fortunately entered the house before this unpleasant interruption, had sat down to breakfast with the rest, when she complained of a sudden indisposition and retired to her room. Her prolonged absence having caused some comment, her father followed her, but learned from her maid that she had only come up to her chamber for an instant, caught up an ulster and bonnet, and hurried down to the passage. One of the footmen declared that he had seen a lady leave the house thus appareled, but had refused to credit that it was his mistress, believing her to be with the company. On ascertaining that his daughter had disappeared, Mr. Aloysius Doran, in conjunction with the bridegroom, instantly put themselves in communication with the police, and very energetic inquiries are being made, which will probably result in a speedy clearing up of this very singular business. Up to a late hour last night, however, nothing had transpired as to the whereabouts of the missing lady. There are rumors of foul play in the matter, and it is said that the police have caused the arrest of the woman who had caused the original disturbance, in the belief that, from jealousy or some other motive, she may have been concerned in the strange disappearance of the bride."

15. What can you infer from this passage?

_____

_____

16.   Name three characters who attended the ceremony.

_____

_____

17.   Read the following sentence from the passage:

It was only after a painful and prolonged scene that she was ejected by the butler and the footman.

Using context clues, write similar words to the following.

a. prolonged: _____

b. ejected: _____

c. footman: _____

18.   What did the writer mean in this sentence? Discuss your answer with a classmate.

There are rumors of foul play in the matter, and it is said that the police have caused the arrest of the woman who had caused the original disturbance, in the belief that, from jealousy or some other motive, she may have been concerned in the strange disappearance of the bride."

_____

_____

19.   PART A

What narrative point of view has been used in the following sentence? Is it first-person or third-person?

The bride, who had fortunately entered the house before this unpleasant interruption, had sat down to breakfast with the rest, when she complained of a sudden indisposition and retired to her room.

_____

PART B- Rewrite the sentence in the narrative point of view you did not choose.

_____

REFLECTION ON LEARNING

Answer the following reflection questions, and feel free to discuss your responses with your teacher or classmate.

- What reading idea or strategy did you learn from this section?

- What new concepts did you learn?

- What methods did you work on in this section?

- What aspect of this section is still not 100 percent clear for you?

- What do you want your teacher to know?

LESSON 14
FINAL THOUGHTS

Congratulations on reaching the end of the lessons. In each lesson, you looked at three main areas: vocabulary, reading comprehension skills and higher-order reading skills. Before you finish, below are some final thoughts:

1. Your success at work and in life depends on your reading skills and habits. The more you read, the more successful you will be.

2. Read with a purpose. Keep in mind what you want to find out and read to get it.

3. Skim through the text to glance at the main idea of the passage, then read it again.

4. Use background knowledge and connect life experiences to your reading. This makes it easier to understand the text.

5. Take as many breaks as you can.

6. Manage your time wisely.

7. Avoid practicing bad habits, such as skipping text and assuming inferences.

8. Practice good reading strategies until they become second nature to you.

9. Above all, read every day. Read all kinds of text. Sharpen your reading skills as if your life depended on it.

Here's a section where you can reflect on how far you have come:

1. What have you learned about reading?

_____

_____

_____

2. Do you think you have improved your reading skills?

_____

_____

_____

ASSESSMENT

READING PRACTICE TEST I

You will read multiple passages and answer 40 questions.

Your test time will be about 1 minute 44 seconds per question.

Your total time for this test is one hour (60 minutes).

Read this passage and answer questions 1 to 6.

Commodore Perry's Expedition to Japan by Adena Barnette

The United States experienced extensive economic and geographical expansion during the 1840s, as the spirit of Manifest Destiny drove Americans west across the North American continent to exert their influence over new places and peoples. Influenced by this expansionary philosophy, political leaders sought to expand American trade relationships worldwide. One of the first targets of this campaign was to open diplomatic and trade relations with isolationist Japan, which had been closed to western traders for centuries. In 1852, President Millard Fillmore ordered Commodore Matthew C. Perry to lead an expedition to secure Japanese trade and access to Japan's ports for American ships.

Perry's fleet, the Susquehanna, Mississippi, Plymouth, *and* Saratoga, *carried 400 sailors and arrived in Edo Bay, today's Tokyo Bay, on July 8, 1853. Upon arrival, Commodore Perry asserted his military authority to intimidate the Japanese into negotiations. For example, Perry refused to speak with any Japanese officials who did not seem to be of high enough rank. When they disembarked on July 14, Perry delivered a letter from President Fillmore to the emperor of Japan describing American interests in opening trade and outlining mutual benefits. Perry and his fleet departed for several months to allow the Japanese to consider the trade proposal.*

1. **PART A**
Which of the following summarizes the main idea of the passage?

A. North America expanded its trade relationships with Japan.

B. North America expanded its rule over Korea.

C. South America expanded its trade relationships with Japan.

D. North America sold its ships to Japan.

PART B

Which of the following sentences from the passage supports your answer to PART A?

A. Perry and his fleet departed for several months to allow the Japanese to consider the trade proposal.

B. Influenced by this expansionary philosophy, political leaders sought to expand American trade relationships worldwide.

C. Upon arrival, Commodore Perry asserted his military authority to intimidate the Japanese into negotiations.

D. The United States experienced extensive economic and geographical expansion during the 1840s, as the spirit of Manifest Destiny drove Americans west across the North American continent to exert their influence over new places and peoples.

2. What did the letter from President Fillmore contain?

A. America's interest in trading with Japan
B. America's interest in conquering Japan

C. America's interest in sailing
D. America's interest in buying ships

3. **PART A**
What is Edo Bay known as today?

A. Kedo Bay
C. Seoul Bay

B. Japan Bay
D. Tokyo Bay

PART B

When did Commodore Perry's fleet land in Japan?

A. 1823

B. 1883

C. 1853

D. 1583

4. Which of the following character traits summarizes Commodore Perry's approach once he landed in Japan?

A. Understanding

B. Authoritative

C. Arrogant

D. Forgiving

5. **PART A**

What is the meaning of the word **isolationist** as used in this excerpt from the passage?

> One of the first targets of this campaign was to open diplomatic and trade relations with **isolationist** Japan, which had been closed to western traders for centuries.

A. Favoring a policy of working with other groups

B. Favoring a policy of remaining apart from the affairs or interests of other groups

C. Favoring a policy of conquering other groups

D. Favoring a policy that includes everyone's interests

PART B

Using a text-to-world connection, what do you think happened after Perry's fleet left for a few months?

A. Trading discussions commenced.

B. There was some reluctance from Japan.

C. A war ensued.

D. Commodore Perry did not return to Japan.

6. Which of the following was not part of Commodore Perry's fleet?

A. Susquehanna

B. Mississippi

C. Plymouth

D. Southside

Read this excerpt from *The Jungle Book* by Rudyard Kipling (1894) and answer 7 to 12.

> All that is told here happened some time before Mowgli was turned out of the Seeonee Wolf Pack, or revenged himself on Shere Khan the tiger. It was in the days when Baloo was teaching him the Law of the Jungle. The big, serious, old brown bear was delighted to have so quick a pupil, for the young wolves will only learn as much of the Law of the Jungle as applies to their own pack and tribe, and run away as soon as they can repeat the Hunting Verse—"Feet that make no noise: eyes that can see in the dark: ears that can hear the winds in their lairs, and sharp white teeth, all these things are the marks of our brothers except Tabaqui the Jackal and the Hyaena whom we hate." But Mowgli, as a man-cub, had to learn a great deal more than this.

Sometimes Bagheera the Black Panther would come lounging through the jungle to see how his pet was getting on, and would purr with his head against a tree while Mowgli recited the day's lesson to Baloo. The boy could climb almost as well as he could swim, and swim almost as well as he could run. So Baloo, the Teacher of the Law, taught him the Wood and Water Laws: how to tell a rotten branch from a sound one: how to speak politely to the wild bees when he came upon a hive of them fifty feet above ground: what to say to Mang the Bat when he disturbed him in the branches at midday: and how to warn the water-snakes in the pools before he splashed down among them. None of the Jungle People like being disturbed, and all are very ready to fly at an intruder. Then, too, Mowgli was taught the Strangers' Hunting Call, which must be repeated aloud till it is answered, whenever one of the Jungle-People hunts outside his own grounds. It means, translated, "Give me leave to hunt here because I am hungry." And the answer is, "Hunt then for food, but not for pleasure."

7. What did the writer mean in this sentence?

But Mowgli, as a man-cub, had to learn a great deal more than this.

A. Mowgli is a tiger.
B. Mowgli is a human child.

C. Mowgli is a human adult.
D. Mowgli is a lion.

8. **PART A**

Which of the following statements describes the main idea of the passage?

A. The lessons Baloo learned
B. The lessons Mowgli learned

C. The lessons Bagheera learned
D. The lessons Bagheera taught

PART B

Which of the following sentences from the passage best supports your answer to PART A?

A. Sometimes Bagheera the Black Panther would come lounging through the jungle to see how his pet was getting on, and would purr with his head against a tree while Mowgli recited the day's lesson to Baloo.
B. It was in the days when Baloo was teaching him the Law of the Jungle.

C. So Baloo, the Teacher of the Law, taught him the Wood and Water Laws
D. None of the Jungle People like being disturbed, and all are very ready to fly at an intruder.

9. What did the writer mean in this excerpt from the passage?

The boy could climb almost as well as he could swim, and swim almost as well as he could run.

A. Mowgli could climb, swim and run in almost equal measure.
B. Mowgli could only run and swim, and struggled to climb.

C. Mowgli could only climb and swim, and struggled to run.
D. Mowgli struggled to run, swim and climb.

10. **PART A**

What would happen if the Jungle-People hunted outside their own grounds?

A. Mowgli would run away.
B. Baloo would need to sound the Stranger's Hunting Call.

C. The Jungle-People would need to sound the Stranger's Hunting Call.
D. Mowgli would need to sound the Human's Hunting Call.

PART B

How long should the sound last?

A. It should be repeated aloud all day.
B. It should be repeated aloud even if it is answered.

C. It should be repeated aloud until it is answered.
D. Never

11. **PART A**

What character trait does the pupil display?

> *The big, serious, old brown bear was delighted to have **so quick** a pupil...*

A. Small
B. Angry

C. Slow learner
D. Fast learner

PART B

Who was the writer referring to?

A. Baloo
B. Bagheera

C. Mowgll
D. Jungle-People

12. Which of the following is a law of the Jungle?

A. The Hunting Verse
B. How to tell a rotten branch from a sound one

C. How to respect Bagheera
D. How to warn the water-snakes in the pools

13. What conclusion can you draw from the following sentence?

> *The wait was going to be long. But the voters stood their ground and waited. They were eager to get their voices heard.*

A. They were planning a riot.
B. Voting was happening the next day.

C. The votes were being counted.
D. The voters were interested in casting their elections.

Read the following poem, "Phantasmagoria and Other Poems: Canto VI – Dyscomfyture" by Lewis Carroll (1911), and answer questions 14 to 17.

> *As one who strives a hill to climb,*
> *Who never climbed before:*
> *Who finds it, in a little time,*
> *Grow every moment less sublime,*
> *And votes the thing a bore:*
> *Yet, having once begun to try,*
> *Dares not desert his quest,*
> *But, climbing, ever keeps his eye*
> *On one small hut against the sky*
> *Wherein he hopes to rest:*

> *Who climbs till nerve and force are spent,*
> *With many a puff and pant:*
> *Who still, as rises the ascent,*
> *In language grows more violent,*
> *Although in breath more scant:*
> *Who, climbing, gains at length the place*
> *That crowns the upward track.*
> *And, entering with unsteady pace,*
> *Receives a buffet in the face*
> *That lands him on his back:*

14. In the first stanza, which word has been used to rhyme with "bore"?

A. sublime
B. before

C. bore
D. time

15. **PART A**

Which of the following describes the main idea in the poem?

A. A man climbing a hill
B. A man thinking of climbing a hill

C. A man becoming tired of walking
D. A man with an unquenchable thirst

PART B

Which of the following supports your answer to PART A?

A. *That crowns the upward track*
B. *As one who strives a hill to climb*

C. *And votes the thing a bore*
D. *On one small hut against the sky*

16. What did the poet mean in this line from the poem?

> *With many a puff and pant:*

A. The man was energetic.
B. The man was inconsiderate.

C. The man was trying to run.
D. The man was out of breath.

17. **PART A**

What does the word **unsteady** mean in this excerpt from the poem?

> *And, entering with **unsteady** pace,/ Receives a buffet in the face*

A. Erratic
B. Steady

C. Straightforward
D. Joyful

PART B

What emotion can you infer from this excerpt?

A. The man was happy.
B. The man was angry.

C. The man was struggling.
D. The man was energetic.

18. Read the following sentence:

> *When Drew hit the baseball, he had no idea where it would have landed.*

If the sentence started in the following way, which of the options would fit?

> *"Drew had no idea where the ball was going to land..."*

A. After he hit the ball.
B. When he hit it.
C. While hitting it.
D. When the ball was hit.

19. Read the following sentence:

> *Carlos Lo has three cats and two dogs. They are all brown, but one of the cats has white spots too. One of the dogs is called Lola.*

Which of the following statements is true?

A. Carlos Lo only has three animals.
B. One of Carlos Lo's cats is named Lola.

C. Carlos Lo has two cats.
D. One of Carlos Lo's cats has white spots.

20. Read the following sentence:

*Yesterday was my son's third birthday. There was a clown who pulled **silly** faces to make everyone laugh.*

What does the word **silly** mean in this sentence?

A. funny

B. tricky

C. scary

D. bad

Read this excerpt from *Little Women* by Louisa May Alcott (1869) and answer questions 21 to 25.

The short afternoon wore away. All other errands were done, and Meg and her mother busy at some necessary needlework, while Beth and Amy got tea, and Hannah finished her ironing with what she called a 'slap and a bang', but still Jo did not come. They began to get anxious, and Laurie went off to find her, for no one knew what freak Jo might take into her head. He missed her, however, and she came walking in with a very queer expression of countenance, for there was a mixture of fun and fear, satisfaction and regret In it, which puzzled the family as much as did the roll of hills she laid before her mother, saying with a little choke in her voice, "That's my contribution toward making Father comfortable and bringing him home!"

"My dear, where did you get it? Twenty-five dollars! Jo, I hope you haven't done anything rash?"

"No, it's mine honestly. I didn't beg, borrow, or steal it. I earned it, and I don't think you'll blame me, for I only sold what was my own."

As she spoke, Jo took off her bonnet, and a general outcry arose, for all her abundant hair was cut short.

"Your hair! Your beautiful hair! Oh, Jo, how could you? Your one beauty. My dear girl, there was no need of this."

"She doesn't look like my Jo anymore, but I love her dearly for it!"

As everyone exclaimed, and Beth hugged the cropped head tenderly, Jo assumed an indifferent air, which did not deceive anyone a particle, and said, rumpling up the brown bush and trying to look as if she liked it, "It doesn't affect the fate of the nation, so don't wail, Beth. It will be good for my vanity; I was getting too proud of my wig. It will do my brains good to have that mop taken off. My head feels deliciously light and cool, and the barber said I could soon have a curly crop, which will be boyish, becoming, and easy to keep in order. I'm satisfied, so please take the money and let's have supper."

21. **PART A**

Which of the following statements summarizes the main idea of the passage?

A. Jo made a contribution of $25.

B. Jo's father recovered.

C. Jo helped her sister Beth.

D. Jo chopped off her hair as a sign of rebellion.

PART B

Which of the following sentences from the passage supports your answer to PART A?

A. "... I'm satisfied, so please take the money and let's have supper."

B. They began to get anxious, and Laurie went off to find her, for no one knew what freak Jo might take into her head.

C. "My dear, where did you get it? Twenty-five dollars! Jo, I hope you haven't done anything rash?"

D. As she spoke, Jo took off her bonnet, and a general outcry arose, for all her abundant hair was cut short.

22. **PART A**

How many characters are present in this scene?

A. 2

B. 7

C. 4

D. 9

PART B

Who went out to look for Jo?

A. Beth

B. Amy

C. Meg

D. Laurie

23. Read the following sentence:

*.... she came walking in with a very **queer** expression of countenance, for there was a mixture of fun and fear, satisfaction, and regret in it...*

What does the word **queer** mean in this sentence?

A. happy

B. angry

C. strange

D. sleepy

24. **PART A**

What do you infer from this excerpt from the passage?

As everyone exclaimed, and Beth hugged the cropped head tenderly, Jo assumed an indifferent air, which did not deceive anyone a particle, and said, rumpling up the brown bush and trying to look as if she liked it...

A. Jo liked her new look.

B. Beth didn't like the new hairdo.

C. Jo was pretending to like her new look.

D. Jo wanted to cry.

PART B

Do you think the other characters believed her?

A. Yes

B. No

C. Maybe

D. I don't know.

25. Read the following sentence from the passage:

"That's my contribution toward making Father comfortable and bringing him home!"

What character trait does Jo show in this sentence?

A. A team player

B. Judgmental

C. Angry

D. Bitter

Read this excerpt from an article titled "The Awakening" by Kate Chopin to answer 26 to 31.

Kate Chopin's novel has been called a scandalous masterpiece. It shocked readers when it was published in 1899, but today it is recognized as an American classic. Born into a wealthy family in St. Louis, Chopin moved to Louisiana when she married at age 20: like many of her other works, The Awakening portrays the Creole elite of Natchitoches parish. In the novel, "Creole" refers to people descended from French and Spanish colonists who settled in Louisiana before it became part of the United States. While Creole people could be white, mixed-race, or black, Creole society maintained a racial hierarchy that privileged light skin. Several of Chopin's works criticize this hierarchy, yet The Awakening largely leaves it unexamined.

To depict Creole culture, Chopin drew inspiration from both American regionalist writers such as Sarah Orne Jewett and French naturalist writers, including Guy de Maupassant. Her writing combines features from both styles, blending regionalism's attention to the features that distinguish American people and places with the objective point of view and occasional pessimism found in naturalism.

The Awakening explores the experience of Edna Pontellier, who chafes against expectations of women in Creole society. Edna's search for an identity beyond marriage and motherhood creates conflict with her husband Léonce, who does not understand her need for independence: this conflict contributes to her affairs with other men. Two other characters, Adèle Ratignolle and Mademoiselle Reisz, serve as foils to Edna. Ratignolle is an example of the idealized Creole woman, living a life completely devoted to a husband and children, while Reisz is single and lives on the margins of society. Together these two reflect the limited options available to women. Dissatisfied and wanting something else, Edna commits suicide to escape these constraints. In spite of its tragic ending, The Awakening is a remarkable portrait of female rebellion. In it, Chopin challenges gender inequalities and questions the social norms that restrict what women like Edna can do and be.

26. **PART A**

Which of the following statements summarizes the main idea of the passage?

A. Kate Chopin's temperament

B. Kate Chopin's outlook on life

C. What Kate Chopin's book is about

D. Kate Chopin's career

PART B

Which of the following sentences from the passage supports your answer to PART A?

A. "The Awakening" explores the experience of Edna Pontellier, who chafes against expectations of women in Creole society.

B. Kate Chopin's novel has been called a scandalous masterpiece.

C. Her writing combines features from both styles, blending regionalism's attention to the features that distinguish American people and places with the objective point of view and occasional pessimism found in naturalism.

D. In spite of its tragic ending, "The Awakening" is a remarkable portrait of female rebellion.

27. **PART A**

Where is Kate Chopin originally from?

A. St. Louis

B. Louisiana

C. New York

D. Manchester

PART B

When did she move?

A. When she was 50.

B. When she was 30.

C. When she was 10.

D. When she was 20.

28. Who is the main character in "The Awakening"?

A. Kate Chopin
B. Edna Pontellier

C. Adèle Ratignolle
D. Mademoiselle Reisz

29. **PART A**

What is the main theme of "The Awakening"?

A. Challenging sexist stereotypes
B. Challenging political laws
C. Praising America's progressive economy
D. Kate Chopin's life story

PART B

Which French naturalist writers did Chopin draw inspiration from?

A. Adèle Ratignolle
B. Mademoiselle Reisz
C. Guy de Maupassant
D. Sarah Orne Jewett

30. Who was privileged in the Creole society?

A. Light-skinned people
B. Americans

C. French
D. Dark-skinned people

31. Which of the following options explains why the main character has affairs?

A. Being abused
B. Being undermined in the society

C. Conflict with her friends
D. Conflict with her husband

Read Edgar Allan Poe's poem "The Bells" to answer questions 32 to 35.

I.

Hear the sledges with the bells—
Silver bells!
What a world of merriment their melody foretells!
How they tinkle, tinkle, tinkle,
In the icy air of night!
While the stars that over sprinkle
All the heavens, seem to twinkle
With a crystalline delight:
Keeping time, time, time,
In a sort of Runic rhyme,
To the tintinnabulation that so musically wells
From the bells, bells, bells, bells,
Bells, bells, bells—
From the jingling and the tinkling of the bells.

II.

Hear the mellow wedding bells,
Golden bells!
What a world of happiness their harmony foretells?
Through the balmy air of night
How they ring out their delight!
From the molten-golden notes,
And all in tune,
What a liquid ditty floats
To the turtle-dove that listens, while she gloats
On the moon!
Oh, from out the sounding cells,
What a gush of euphony voluminously wells!
How it swells!
How it dwells
On the Future! how it tells
Of the rapture that impels
To the swinging and the ringing
Of the bells, bells, bells,
Of the bells, bells, bells, bells,
Bells, bells, bells—
To the rhyming and the chiming of the bells!

32. What type of figurative language has been used in the following sentence from the passage?

What a world of merriment their melody foretells!

    A. Simile
    B. Hyperbole

    C. Alliteration
    D. Metaphor

33. **PART A**
What type of bells are ringing in the second stanza?

    A. Wedding bells
    B. Silver sleigh bells
    C. Alarm bells
    D. Ambulance bells

PART B
What type of emotion is being inferred in this stanza?

    A. Happiness
    B. Sadness
    C. Bitterness
    D. Anger

34. In the first stanza, which word rhymes with "tinkle"?

    A. time
    C. wells

    B. tinkle
    D. sprinkle

35. What do you think the word **balmy** means in this sentence?

*Through the **balmy** air of night...*

    A. harsh
    B. pleasant

    C. draining
    D. hot

Use the data from the bar graph to answer questions 36 to 38.

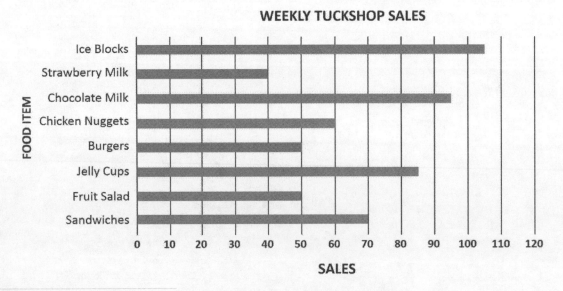

36. **PART A**
What is the least popular item?

    A. Fruit salad
    B. Burgers

    C. Sandwiches
    D. Strawberry milk

PART B

How many were sold during the week?

A.	50	C.	40
B.	50	D.	70

37. What season do you think the Tuckshop owner makes the most profit?

A. Winter	C. Summer
B. Spring	D. Autumn

38. How many jelly cups were sold during the week?

A. 85	C. 100
B. 120	D. 80

39. **PART A**

Which sentence is written in the first-person narration?

A. I looked to the sky and saw a bird flying away from the commotion.

B. She understood what the mayor was saying.

C. Kelly wanted to go for a late-night drive to cool down.

D. They told the storeowner they wanted more flavors to be stocked.

PART B

Which of the following is a third-person rewrite of the sentence you chose in PART A?

A. I wanted to go for a late-night drive to cool down.

B. "We want more flavors to be stocked," I told the store owner.

C. Violet looked to the sky and saw a bird flying away from the commotion.

D. "I understand what you are saying, Mayor," I replied.

40. What does the word **tangible** mean in this sentence?

> "I'd rather you make **tangible** promises, rather than telling me what I want to hear," Fred responded to the plumber.

A. actual	C. shady
B. edible	D. basic

ASSESSMENT

READING PRACTICE TEST II

You will read multiple passages and answer 40 questions.
Your test time will be about 1 minute 44 seconds per question.
Your total time for this test is one hour (60 minutes).

Read this excerpt from *Black Beauty* by Anna Sewell (1877) to answer questions 1 to 5.

As soon as my knees were sufficiently healed I was turned into a small meadow for a month or two: no other creature was there: and though I enjoyed the liberty and the sweet grass, yet I had been so long used to society that I felt very lonely. Ginger and I had become fast friends, and now I missed her company extremely. I often neighed when I heard horses' feet passing in the road, but I seldom got an answer: till one morning the gate was opened, and who should come in but dear old Ginger. The man slipped off her halter, and left her there. With a joyful whinny I trotted up to her: we were both glad to meet, but I soon found that it was not for our pleasure that she was brought to be with me. Her story would be too long to tell, but the end of it was that she had been ruined by hard riding, and was now turned off to see what rest would do.

Lord George was young and would take no warning: he was a hard rider, and would hunt whenever he could get the chance, quite careless of his horse. Soon after I left the stable there was a steeplechase, and he determined to ride. Though the groom told him she was a little strained, and was not fit for the race, he did not believe it, and on the day of the race urged Ginger to keep up with the foremost riders. With her high spirit, she strained herself to the utmost: she came in with the first three horses, but her wind was touched, besides which he was too heavy for her, and her back was strained. "And so," she said, "here we are, ruined in the prime of our youth and strength, you by a drunkard, and I by a fool: it is very hard." We both felt in ourselves that we were not what we had been. However, that did not spoil the pleasure we had in each other's company: we did not gallop about as we once did, but we used to feed, and lie down together, and stand for hours under one of the shady lime-trees with our heads close to each other: and so we passed our time till the family returned from town.

1. PART A

Which of the following statements summarize the main idea of the passage?

A. The characters' owners put them to work.

B. The characters' owners were hard riders.

C. The characters enjoy each other's company.

D. The characters' owners left them alone.

PART B

Which of the following sentences from the passage supports your answer to PART A?

A. However, that did not spoil the pleasure we had in each other's company: we did not gallop about as we once did, but we used to feed, and lie down together...

B. Ginger and I had become fast friends, and now I missed her company extremely.

C. With a joyful whinny, I trotted up to her: we were both glad to meet, but I soon found that it was not for our pleasure that she was brought to be with me.

D. With her high spirit, she strained herself to the utmost...

2. What is the meaning of the word **liberty** in the following sentence from the excerpt?

*...and though I enjoyed the **liberty** and the sweet grass...*

A. happiness   C. freedom

B. instability   D. restriction

3. What emotion is being inferred in this sentence?

   We both felt in ourselves that we were not what we had been.

   A. longing   C. bitter
   B. anger   D. joy

4. PART A
What type of animal is the character?

   A. human   C. rat
   B. cow   D. horse

PART B
Which of the following sentences from the passage **does not** support your answer to PART A?

A. I often neighed when I heard horses' feet passing in the road, but I seldom got an answer...

B. ...and so we passed our time till the family returned from town.

C. With a joyful whinny, I trotted up to her: we were both glad to meet...

D. Soon after I left the stable there was a steeplechase, and he determined to ride.

5. What character trait does Ginger portray in this sentence from the excerpt?

   With her high spirit, she strained herself to the utmost: she came in with the first three horses, but her wind was touched, besides which he was too heavy for her, and her back was strained.

A. perseverance   C. anger
B. stubbornness   D. caution

6. Which of the following linking words could be used to connect the two sentences below?

   Monica didn't have time to go to the supermarket. There was no bread in the fridge.

   A. however   C. although
   B. consequently   D. in addition

7. What are the root words in the following sentences?

   a. hopping: _____

   b. undo: _____

   c. lovely: _____

   d. unstoppable: _____

8. Which of the following linking words can be used to connect the two sentences below?

   Attendees should be quiet during the music concert. Applause at the end is allowed.

   A. otherwise   C. although
   B. furthermore   D. similarly

The following graph represents sales from two stores. The lighter grey represents Chad's store, while the darker grey represents Carol's. Use the data to answer questions 9 to 13.

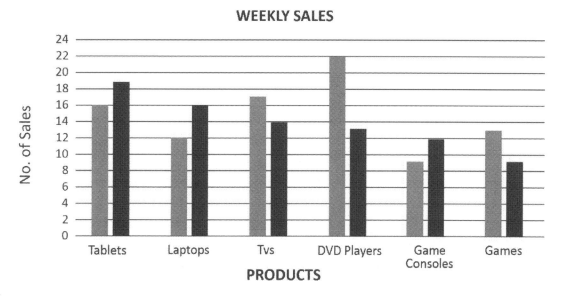

9. How many laptops did Carol's store sell?

    A. 14   C. 12

    B. 16   D. 13

10. Which item was sold the most in Chad's store?

    A. Tablets   C. Games

    B. TVs   D. DVD players

11. **PART A**

Why do you think game consoles sold the least in both stores?

    A. They are cheap.

    B. They are expensive.

    C. They are rare.

    D. They are popular.

PART B

How many game consoles did Carol sell?

    A. 13

    B. 14

    C. 15

    D. 12

12. How many more games did Chad's store sell than Carol's?

    A. 13   C. 5

    B. 8   D. 4

13. Why do you think such data is collected?

    A. To see how many sales have been made   C. To know which items are popular

    B. To see what should be advertised   D. All of the above

Read the following excerpt from *Gulliver's Travels into Several Remote Nations of the World* by Jonathan Swift (1926) to answer questions 14 to 18.

> *When they began to talk, I thought I never heard or saw anything more unnatural: for it appeared to me as monstrous as if a dog or a cow should speak in England, or a Yahoo in Houyhnhnmland. The honest Portuguese were equally amazed at my strange dress, and the odd manner of delivering my words, which, however, they understood very well. They spoke to me with great humanity, and said, "they were sure the captain would carry me gratis to Lisbon, whence I might return to my own country: that two of the seamen would go back to the ship, inform the captain of what they had seen, and receive his orders: in the meantime, unless I would give my solemn oath not to fly, they would secure me by force." I thought it best to comply with their proposal. They were very curious to know my story, but I gave them very little satisfaction, and they all conjectured that my misfortunes had impaired my reason. In two hours the boat, which went laden with vessels of water, returned, with the captain's command to fetch me on board. I fell on my knees to preserve my liberty: but all was in vain: and the men, having tied me with cords, heaved me into the boat, whence I was taken into the ship, and thence into the captain's cabin.*
>
> *His name was Pedro de Mendez: he was a very courteous and generous person. He entreated me to give some account of myself, and desired to know what I would eat or drink: said, "I should be used as well as himself:" and spoke so many obliging things, that I wondered to find such civilities from a Yahoo. However, I remained silent and sullen: I was ready to faint at the very smell of him and his men.*
>
> *At last I desired something to eat out of my own canoe: but he ordered me a chicken, and some excellent wine, and then directed that I should be put to bed in a very clean cabin. I would not undress myself, but lay on the bed-clothes, and in half an hour stole out, when I thought the crew was at dinner, and getting to the side of the ship, was going to leap into the sea, and swim for my life, rather than continue among Yahoos. But one of the seamen prevented me, and having informed the captain, I was chained to my cabin.*

14. **PART A**

Which of the following statements summarize the main idea of the passage?

A. The main character was abducted.

B. The main character wanted to get on a boat.

C. The main character knew where he was.

D. The main character liked the sea.

PART B

Which of the following sentences from the passage supports your answer to PART A?

A. In two hours the boat, which went laden with vessels of water, returned, with the captain's command to fetch me on board.

B. But one of the seamen prevented me, and having informed the captain, I was chained to my cabin.

C. I fell on my knees to preserve my liberty: but all was in vain: and the men, having tied me with cords, heaved me into the boat, whence I was taken into the ship, and thence into the captain's cabin.

D. When they began to talk, I thought I never heard or saw anything more unnatural.

15. **PART A**

What did the writer mean in this sentence?

> *They were very curious to know my story, but I gave them very little satisfaction, and they all <u>conjectured</u> that my misfortunes had impaired my reason.*

A. The main character defended himself.

B. The main character was silent as the other characters talked about him.

C. The main character was listening to the other characters' stories.

D. The main character was in pain.

PART B

What does the word **conjectured** mean as used in the sentence in Part A?

A. fought

B. ran

C. yelled

D. guessed

16. What did the writer mean in this sentence?

> *I was ready to faint at the very smell of him and his men.*

A. The characters were hungry.

B. The main character smelled bad.

C. The characters smelled bad.

D. The main character was hungry.

17. Which of the following options is similar to the word **gratis**?

> *...they were sure the captain would carry me **gratis** to Lisbon, whence I might return to my own country...*

A. without charge

B. without restraint

C. to freedom

D. with a fee

18. **PART A**

How many seamen talked to the captain?

A. 4

B. 5

C. 2

D. 8

PART B

What did the main character think about the captain?

A. The main character was angered by the captain.

B. The main character thought he was arrogant.

C. The main character thought the captain was polite.

D. The main character was in love with the captain.

19. Which of the following is an example of a direct characterization?

A. Fred's shyness often prevented him from going to parties.

B. Although it was midnight, Molly knew that if she continued working for a little longer her work would be perfect.

C. "Thank you for escorting me to my door," said Ahmed.

D. Turner walked up to the new girl in class and said, "Welcome to East High!"

20. Can you predict what happens in the following story?

> *"Hey! Do you want me to help you study?" Paulina's mom asked.*
>
> *"I don't know," Paulina replied. "I went through the list three times last night. I think I can spell all the words."*
>
> *"Better safe than sorry," Paulina's mom said. "And you have plenty of time before the bus comes."*
> *Paulina handed her word list to her mom.*

A. Paulina made a sandwich for her lunch.

B. Paulina was late for the school bus.

C. Paulina put the spelling word list in her backpack.

D. Paulina's mom quizzed her on the spelling words.

Read the following excerpt from *The Adventures of Tom Sawyer* by Mark Twain (1876) to answer 21 to 26.

The raft drew beyond the middle of the river: the boys pointed her head right, and then lay on their oars. The river was not high, so there was not more than a two or three mile current. Hardly a word was said during the next three-quarters of an hour. Now the raft was passing before the distant town. Two or three glimmering lights showed where it lay, peacefully sleeping, beyond the vague vast sweep of star-gemmed water, unconscious of the tremendous event that was happening.

The Black Avenger stood still with folded arms, "looking his last" upon the scene of his former joys and his later sufferings, and wishing "she" could see him now, abroad on the wild sea, facing peril and death with dauntless heart, going to his doom with a grim smile on his lips. It was but a small strain on his imagination to remove Jackson's Island beyond eye-shot of the village, and so he "looked his last" with a broken and satisfied heart. The other pirates were looking their last, too: and they all looked so long that they came near letting the current drift them out of the range of the island. But they discovered the danger in time, and made shift to avert it. About two o'clock in the morning the raft grounded on the bar two hundred yards above the head of the island, and they waded back and forth until they had landed their freight. Part of the little raft's belongings consisted of an old sail, and this they spread over a nook in the bushes for a tent to shelter their provisions: but they themselves would sleep in the open air in good weather, as became outlaws. They built a fire against the side of a great log twenty or thirty steps within the somber depths of the forest, and then cooked some bacon in the frying-pan for supper, and used up half of the corn "pone" stock they had brought. It seemed glorious sport to be feasting in that wild, freeway in the virgin forest of an unexplored and uninhabited island, far from the haunts of men, and they said they never would return to civilization. The climbing fire lit up their faces and threw its ruddy glare upon the pillared tree-trunks of their forest temple, and upon the varnished foliage and festooning vines.

21. PART A

Which of the following statements describes the main idea of the passage?

A. The characters' journey from the village to the island

B. The characters' forgetfulness

C. The characters' relationship with each other

D. The characters becoming pirates

PART B

Which of the following sentences from the passage supports your answer to PART A?

A. Now the raft was passing before the distant town.

B. The other pirates were looking their last, too: and they all looked so long that they came near letting the current drift them out of the range of the island.

C. Part of the little raft's belongings consisted of an old sail, and this they spread over a nook in the bushes for a tent to shelter their provisions...

D. It was but a small strain on his imagination to remove Jackson's Island beyond eye-shot of the village, and so he "looked his last" with a broken and satisfied heart.

22. How many minutes are being referred to in this sentence?

*Hardly a word was said during the next **three-quarters of an hour.***

A. 15 minutes

B. 30 minutes

C. 5 minutes

D. 45 minutes

23. How high was the river tide?

    A. Between four and five miles
    C. Above five miles

    B. Between two or three miles
    D. Below two miles

24. **PART A**

Why did the characters erect a tent?

    A. To sleep in
    B. To shelter from the incoming rain
    C. To shelter their provisions
    D. For safety

PART B

What did the writer compare their sleeping decision to?

    A. Sleeping outside like outlaws
    B. Sleeping hurdled together for warmth
    C. Sleeping outside like in-laws
    D. Sleeping hurdled away from each other

25. **PART A**

What can you infer from this excerpt from the passage?

It seemed glorious sport to be feasting in that wild, freeway in the virgin forest of an unexplored and <u>uninhabited</u> *island, far from the haunts of men, and they said they never would return to civilization.*

    A. The characters were hating themselves.
    B. The characters were fighting between themselves.
    C. The characters were enjoying their newfound freedom.
    D. The characters were enjoying the food.

PART B

What does the word **uninhabited** mean as used in the excerpt above?

    A. without food
    B. without people
    C. without order
    D. without water

26. What would have happened if the characters had gotten distracted looking at the life they were leaving behind?

    A. The current would have drifted them away from the range of the island.
    B. The current would have drifted them closer to the range of the island.
    C. The current would have swept them away.
    D. The current would have caused them to drown.

Read the following chorus lyrics titled "Mirror" by Lil Wayne and Bruno Mars to answer questions 27 and 28.

Mirror on the wall,

Here we are again,

Through my rise and fall,

You've been only friend,

You told me that they can,

Understand the man I am,

So why are we here,

Talkin' to each other again.

27. What do you think the theme of the song is?

A. Entertaining our friends
B. Escaping daily life struggles
C. Embracing love
D. Reflecting on our decisions in life

28. **PART A**

What is the symbol in the chorus?

A. The mirror
B. A friend
C. Man
D. Talkin'

PART B

What does it symbolize?

A. Our joy and happiness
B. A fulfilled life
C. The darkness and light within us
D. Our perseverance

29. What inference can you make based on the details given in the following paragraph?

Ted left the house, anger boiling within him. He was fed up with having to deal with no hot water in his house. Though he had told his landlord of the problem, nothing had happened. He had had enough. Ted got into his car and drove, determined to resolve the problem today.

A. Ted was heading to an electrician.
B. Ted was heading to the landlord's house.
C. Ted was heading to work.
D. Ted was heading to his friend's house to shower.

30. What is being likened to a **delicate flower** in the sentence below?

"His promise to me was a **delicate flower**," Clare declared.

A. The person who made the promise
B. Clare
C. The promise made by the other person
D. The promise made by Clare

Read the following excerpt from an article titled "Theodore Dreiser's *Sister Carrie* and the Urbanization of Chicago" by Jolie Sheffer to answer questions 31 to 35.

Theodore Herman Albert Dreiser, an influential and at times infamous author of literary naturalism, was born in Terre Haute, Indiana in 1871. The eleventh of thirteen children, he had an unhappy childhood shaped by poverty. At age fifteen, he left home. After several years of menial labor and some college, in 1892 he started as a journalist at the Chicago Globe. Interested in the work of Charles Darwin and Herbert Spencer, Dreiser began writing fiction that explored ideas of social determinism and the "survival of the fittest," particularly during a period of intense urbanization across the country.

Sister Carrie (1900) was Dreiser's first novel, and it reflects the ideas of literary naturalism through its attitude of scientific objectivity toward human behavior. The novel centers on Carrie Meeber, a young woman from rural Wisconsin who moves to Chicago to earn money. First seduced by a traveling salesman on her train ride into the city, Carrie quickly adapts to her new environment, where she learns to make use of other men and the opportunities she encounters. The novel shows the attractions and dangers of big city life in the late nineteenth century, with its glittering department stores, theaters, dance halls, and other opportunities to mingle with the opposite sex without supervision. The novel ends with Carrie becoming a successful stage actress in New York City, while one of her lovers spirals downward and commits suicide.

> *Dreiser's frank treatment of sex and materialism, and his refusal to punish characters for their behavior, shocked readers.* Sister Carrie *was attacked by censors for its immorality, and the book was banned in New York City and Cincinnati in 1916. Dreiser continued to court controversy throughout his career. In 1929 he was subject to an obscenity trial for his bestselling novel* An American Tragedy *(1925). He was increasingly drawn to social justice efforts in the 1930s, including letter-writing campaigns as an anti-war activist, supporting the American Communist Party, and fighting racial injustice in the Scottsboro Boys case.*

31. PART A

Which of the following statements summarizes the main idea of the passage?

A. What the book *Sister Carrie* is about
B. What influenced Dreiser's writing

C. Who wrote *Sister Carrie*
D. The urbanization of Chicago

PART B

Which of the following sentences from the passage supports your answer to PART A?

A. He was increasingly drawn to social justice efforts in the 1930s, including letter-writing campaigns as an anti-war activist, supporting the American Communist Party, and fighting racial injustice in the Scottsboro Boys case.
B. At age fifteen, he left home.

C. *Sister Carrie* (1900) was Dreiser's first novel, and it reflects the ideas of literary naturalism through its attitude of scientific objectivity toward human behavior.
D. Dreiser continued to court controversy throughout his career.

32. Using a text-to-world connection, what do you think is the theme of *Sister Carrie*?

A. Female empowerment
B. Female degradation

C. Freedom to take advantage of people
D. Severe punishment for immoral people

33. PART A

Why was Dreiser's book banned in New York?

A. Because it had vulgar language
B. Because it accused censors of hypocrisy
C. Because it contained immoral acts
D. Because it dehumanized human existence

PART B

What is the name of his other book that caused him to be taken to court?

A. Chicago Globe
B. An American Tragedy
C. American Communist Party
D. Scottsboro Boys

34. PART A

Which newspaper did Dreiser work for?

A. Daily Globe
B. New York Mail
C. Daily Mail
D. Chicago Globe

PART B

What year was he hired to work there?

A. 1882
B. 1982
C. 1992
D. 1892

35. Using a text-to-world connection, why do you think readers were shocked by the contents of *Sister Carrie*?

A. Sex and materialism were considered unusual acts.

B. Sex and materialism were considered immoral acts, and often followed by negative consequences.

C. Sex and materialism were considered immoral acts and punishable by death.

D. The readers expected more content relating to sex and materialism.

Read this excerpt from *The Innocence Of Father Brown* by G. K. Chesterton (1911) to answer questions 36 to 40.

Father Brown, though he knew every detail done behind the scenes, and had even evoked applause by his transformation of a pillow into a pantomime baby, went round to the front and sat among the audience with all the solemn expectation of a child at his first matinee. The spectators were few, relations, one or two local friends, and the servants: Sir Leopold sat in the front seat, his full and still fur-collared figure largely obscuring the view of the little cleric behind him: but it has never been settled by artistic authorities whether the cleric lost much. The pantomime was utterly chaotic, yet not contemptible: there ran through it a rage of improvisation which came chiefly from Crook the clown. Commonly he was a clever man, and he was inspired tonight with a wild omniscience, a folly wiser than the world, that which comes to a young man who has seen for an instant a particular expression on a particular face. He was supposed to be the clown, but he was really almost everything else, the author (so far as there was an author), the prompter, the scene-painter, the scene-shifter, and, above all, the orchestra. At abrupt intervals in the outrageous performance he would hurl himself in full costume at the piano and bang out some popular music equally absurd and appropriate. The climax of this, as of all else, was the moment when the two front doors at the back of the scene flew open, showing the lovely moonlit garden, but showing more prominently the famous professional guest: the great Florian, dressed up as a policeman.

36. What does the word **contemptible** mean as used in the sentence below?

*The pantomime was utterly chaotic, yet not **contemptible**: there ran through it a rage of improvisation which came chiefly from Crook the clown.*

A. Worthy of contempt

B. Worthy of praise

C. Worthy of a second look

D. Worthy of applause

37. What general emotion can you infer from the passage?

A. Confusion

B. Anger

C. Betrayal

D. Surprise

38. **PART A**

What do you think the writer meant in this excerpt from the passage?

> *Sir Leopold sat in the front seat, his full and still fur-collared figure largely obscuring the view of the little cleric behind him: but it has never been settled by artistic authorities whether the cleric lost much.*

A. Though the cleric's view was obscured, there was no one on stage.

B. Though the cleric's view was obscured, there was nothing they were missing out on.

C. The cleric complained to the artistic authorities.

D. The cleric's view was not obscured.

PART B

What impression of Sir Leopold do you get?

A. He was a humble person.

B. He was a considerate person.

C. He was an arrogant person.

D. He was a prominent person.

39. **PART A**

What was Crook the Clown's primary role in the pantomime?

A. Acting like a clown
B. Acting like an audience member
C. Acting like a baby
D. Acting like a woman

PART B

Which of the following is not a role that Crook the Clown had?

A. Scene-painter
B. Playing the music
C. Policeman
D. Prompter

40. **PART A**

What do you infer from the sentence below from the passage?

> *At abrupt intervals in the outrageous performance he would hurl himself in full costume at the piano and bang out some popular music equally **absurd** and appropriate.*

A. The performer is eccentric.
B. The performer is losing his mind.
C. The performer is happy to entertain.
D. The performer is a good dancer.

PART B

Which of the following is similar to the word **absurd** as used in the excerpt above?

A. light-hearted
B. ridiculous

C. Hateful
D. lovable

REFLECTION

Answer the following reflection questions, and feel free to discuss your responses with your teacher or classmate.

- How do you feel about your performance on the practice tests?

- Was anything too hard for you? What was it?

- Was anything too easy for you? What was it?

- What reading strategies do you still need to review?

- What else do you want your teacher to know?

ANSWER KEYS

TEST I	Q	PART A	PART B		Q	PART A	PART B		Q	PART A	PART B
	1	A	B		15	A	B		29	A	C
	2	A			16	D			30	A	
	3	D	C		17	A	C		31	D	
	4	B			18	B			32	C	A
	5	B	B		19	D			33	A	A
	6	D			20	A			34	D	
	7	B			21	A	C		35	B	
	8	B	A		22	B	D		36	D	C
	9	A			23	C			37	C	
	10	C	C		24	C	B		38	A	
	11	D	C		25	A			39	A	C
	12	A			26	C	A		40	A	
	13	D			27	A	D				
	14	B			28	B					

TEST II	Q	PART A	PART B		Q	PART A	PART B		Q	PART A	PART B
	1	C	A		14	A	C		28	A	C
	2	C			15	B	D		29	B	
	3	A			16	C			30	C	
	4	D	B		17	A			31	B	A
	5	A			18	C	C		32	A	
	6	A			19	A			33	C	B
	7	Hop, do, love, stop			20	D			34	D	D
	8	C			21	D	B		35	B	
	9	B			22	D			36	A	
	10	D			23	B			37	A	
	11	B	C		24	C	A		38	B	D
	12	D			25	C	B		39	A	C
	13	D			26	A			40	A	B
					27	D					

ANSWER KEYS FOR THE PRACTICE EXERCISES

LESSON 2
Exercise 1
1. a. The root word "annual" means occurring once per year.
   b. The writer has used the word "biannually" to mean that Charlie celebrates his birthday twice every year.

2. a. The root word "agree" means to have the same opinion about something.
   b. The writer has used the word "disagreed" to mean that Shaun and Lucas did not usually have the same opinion on topics and situations.

Exercise 2

She had not wanted a little girl at all, and when Mary was born she handed her over to the care of an **Ayah (nurse)**, who was made to understand that if she wished to please the **Mem Sahib (madam)** she must keep the child out of sight as much as possible. So when she was a **sickly (ill)**, **fretful (distressed)**, ugly little baby she was kept out of the way, and when she became a sickly, fretful, **toddling (baby)** thing she was kept out of the way also.

Practice Exercise
1. c
2. b
3. b
4. d
5. a
6. c

7. The most incredible thing about **miracles** is that they happen. A few clouds in heaven do come together into the staring shape of one **human** eye. A tree does stand up in the **landscape** of a doubtful journey in the exact and elaborate shape of a note of interrogation. I have seen both these things myself within the last few days. Nelson does die in the instant of victory: and a man named Williams does quite **accidentally** murder a man named Williamson: it sounds like a sort of infanticide. In short, there is in life an element of elfin coincidence which people reckoning on the prosaic may perpetually miss. As it has been well **expressed** in the paradox of Poe, wisdom **should** reckon on the unforeseen.

8.

WORD	PREFIX	ROOT WORD	SUFFIX
Telephone	tele-	phone	
Translation		translate	-ion
Nonsense	non-	sense	
Creation		create	-ion
Inscribe	in-	scribe	
Loveable		love	-able
Autograph	auto-	graph	

9. a. rushed: **done very hurriedly**
   b. conviction: **a strong belief or opinion**
   c. helpless: **to be unable to help or do something on one's own**
   d. imprisoned: **to be kept in a prison**
   e. doubtless: **certainly**

LESSON 3
Exercise 1

1. **Cause:** It was very hot outside.
   Effect: The horses were thirsty.

2. **Cause:** The pot contained too much water.
   Effect: The pot rattled on the stove.

Exercise 2

1. I eat meat, but my partner is a vegetarian.
2. Carlos got an A in math, and he is also doing well in other subjects.

Exercise 3

1. The robin used to take short flights of a few yards.
2. The robin mentioned to his friend that he observed a boy learning to walk like how he learned how to fly.
3. The robin thinks her Eggs are cleverer than the boy.
4. The robin's friend says that humans are clumsy.

Exercise 4

1. The person prefers sand in their coffee.
2. The person prefers salt in their tea.

Answer may also include:
- The person would like fish-flavored eggs.
- The person does not want a surrounding of grass or trees.
- The person always wants wet feet.

Practice Exercise

1. Christopher Columbus made his first voyage in 1492.
2. During his second voyage, Columbus introduced animals such as horses, dogs, pigs, cattle, chickens, sheep and goats to the "new" world.
3. Alfred Crosby wrote *The Columbian Exchange: Biological and Cultural Consequences of 1492*.
4. The Spanish conquistador and explorer, Francisco Pizarro, brought the potato to Europe.
5. Slavery began when Europeans wanted free labor to work the lands in the Americas.
6. In *Great Expectations*, Dickens describes the man as fearful and abused in various ways as he had been soaked in water, smothered in mud, lamed by stones, cut by flints, stung by nettles

and torn by briars. However, in a *Christmas Carol*, the old man is described without marks of abuse.

Additionally, the old man in *Great Expectations* has been soaked in water and shivers from the cold. However, the man in a *Christmas Carol* seems to emit coldness and make his surroundings cold.

7. In *Great Expectations* and *A Christmas Carol*, Charles Dickens describes two elderly men. The man in *Great Expectations* is fearful and has been beaten and abused. However, Scrooge, the old man in *A Christmas Carol*, is cold-hearted and does not fear anything. While the character in Great Expectations shivers from the coldness he endures, Scrooge *in A Christmas Carol* makes his surroundings cold.

LESSON 4
Exercise 1
Both pictures show people with placards, and they both seem to depict scenes of protests.
The writings on the placards in both pictures urge people to treat others better and recognize basic human rights.

Exercise 2
The picture shows the logos of various social media platforms. It reminds me that we are in the age of social media where people have multiple accounts to connect with others, advertise their businesses and express themselves.

Practice Exercise
1. a. i. I act like Colin when I am curious and wonder what my mother thinks about when she is quiet.
    ii. Ben reminds me of an old man in my neighborhood who speaks roughly but acts kindly toward the children.
    iii. This excerpt reminds me of myself growing up and becoming stronger.

    b. i. The text reminds me of children who have chronic health conditions.
    ii. The text also reminds me of real stories in which persons are healed from severe illnesses or regain the ability to walk after experiencing paralysis.
    iii. The text also reminds me that the human body is capable of miraculous recoveries.

2. a. The picture reminds me that I would have been unable to vote decades ago, but I am now able to exercise my right.
    b. The picture reminds me of how minority groups have been disadvantaged and have had to fight for basic human rights for years.
3. a. The narrator in *A Journal of the Plague Year* seems to be wealthy with a house, store and servants. Contrastingly, the narrator in *Moby Dick* seems to be poorer and without a home.

    b. In *A Journal of the Plague Year*, I am reminded of entrepreneurs and other businesspeople who struggled during the COVID-19 pandemic. I also think of British colonialism in America.

c. When reading *Moby Dick*, I remember the old house where I grew up. I also remember a storm that I experienced recently in which the wind sounded terrifying as it blew down trees.

4. This reminds me of the hours I spend in the library during my final exams.

LESSON 5
Exercise 1
1. Flesh symbolizes mortality and the human body.
2. Green symbolizes envy.
3. A dove with an olive branch symbolizes peace.

Exercise 2
1. The person is extremely exhausted and needs a long rest.
2. The hare's ears were very long.

Exercise 3
By **th**is time, now and **th**en sheering to one side or **the** other to avoid a reef, but still hugging **the** wind and **the** land, we had g**o**t r**ou**nd I**o**na and begun **to** c**o**me al**o**ngside Mull. **The t**ide at **the t**ail of **the** land ran very strong, and **th**rew **the** brig about. Two **h**ands were put to the **h**elm, and **H**oseason **h**imself would sometimes lend a **h**elp: and it was **s**trange to **s**ee three **s**trong men **th**row **th**eir weight upon **the** tiller, and it (**l**ike a **l**iving thing) struggle **a**gainst **a**nd drive them back. **Th**is would have been **the** greater danger had not the sea been for some while free **of o**bstacles. Mr. Riach, besides, announced from **the** top **th**at he saw clear water ahead.
_____
Excerpt from 'Kidnapped' by Robert Louis Stevenson (1886).

Exercise 4
Behemoth **b**iggest **b**orn of earth upheaved
His vastness: **F**leeced the **f**locks and bleating rose,
As plants: **A**mbiguous between sea **a**nd land
The river-horse, and scaly crocodile.

Exercise 5
1. "Drinks like a fish" is the simile.
2. "Slithered like a snake" is the simile.
3. "As thin as a rail" is the simile.
4. "Like a lion" is the simile.

Exercise 6
The singer is comparing the person he loves to a wish that came true. The person is also a "getaway car" because they get him out of trouble, and they are a "swimming pool on an August day" because they comfort him.

Practice Exercise

1. a. The poem reminds me of wildflowers found in the woods.

    b. "**P**ink, small, and **p**unctual;" "**c**overt in April, **c**andid in May;" "**kn**own by the **kn**oll" and "**b**old little **b**eauty, **b**edecked with thee" are examples of alliteration.

2. a. His hands were very long.

    b. His feet were large and strangely shaped.

    c. He seemed like one who had survived great hardship and starvation.

    d. He looked frightening and malnourished.

3. In the speech, the torch represents determination and a passion for freedom. Additionally, the ballot represents women's right to vote. The flag is also symbolic as it represents American patriotism, determination and courage.

4. a. The old bread was as dry as a bone.

    b. The yowling of the cat at night was like the shriek of a banshee.

    c. When she received the news, Jesse's face glowed like the sun.

    d. After eating a huge dinner, Pete's belly was round like a barrel.

    e. Jennifer's bedroom was as messy as a pigsty.

5. It is an example of simile and alliteration.

6. a. The person's dad is being compared to an angry beast.

    b. The lion is being compared to a funny clown.

    c. The teacher is being compared to a bear.

LESSON 6
Practice Exercise

1. b.
-   The characters observe the streets lined with houses and stores built of green marble and emeralds.
-   They walk on a pavement of green marble and emeralds.
-   They observe the people that were wearing green attire.

2. a. The main idea is that some friendships can be difficult and bring sorrow rather than joy.

    b. Evidence of the main idea can be seen in the line, "And must I then, at Friendship's call,/ Calmly resign the little all/ I have of gladness,/ And lend my being to the thrall/ Of gloom and sadness?"

    c. An appropriate title would be "Sorrowful Friendships."

3. a. The main idea is that the audience was impressed by the actors and the backdrop of the play.

    b. One line to support the main idea is "The gruff tones of Hugo's voice, with an occasional shout when his feelings overcame him, were very impressive, and the audience applauded the moment he paused for breath."

c. An appropriate title is "An Impressive Performance."

4. a. The image tells me that bicycles seem to be the main mode of transport in this area.

b. As pollution worsens, humans decide to reduce their carbon emissions drastically by making bicycles their main mode of transport.

c. An appropriate title would be "Reducing Your Carbon Footprint."

d. This picture reminds me of riding my bicycle around my neighborhood.

LESSON 7

1. a. The movie was as exciting as an amusement ride.

b. Jackie and Mason were brave like lions.

c. The coat was wet like a fish.

2. a. Title 1: A Pack of Dogs
    Title 2: The Lone Dog
    b.

-   The dogs were hunting with their owner when the one in "The Lone Dog" became separated and lost.
-   Some stray dogs are chasing a squirrel, and the dog in "The Lone Dog" is observing them from his home.
-   The dog in "The Lone Dog" is the leader of the pack, and he is waiting for the others to catch up on a hunting exhibition.

3. a. Love is what makes life sweet, enjoyable and comforting.

b. My parents are the ones who hold the family together and encourage us to flourish in whatever we do.

c. The snowdrifts look beautiful and shine under the sun.

d. The class is exciting and a place to discover many things.

4. I- G
    II- F
    III- K
    IV- J
    V- L
    VI- E
    VII- B
    VIII- A
    IX- I
    X- H
    XI- D
    XII- C

5.

	WHOLE WORD	ROOT WORD	MEANING OF ROOT WORD
a.	Wonderment	Wonder	A feeling of amazement about something
b.	Development	Develop	To build up
c.	Unlikable	Like	To think of someone or something in a favorable way
d.	Government	Govern	To control or manage
e.	Sincerity	Sincere	To be honest

6.

All the great modern inventions come from the Home of the Scholars, such as the newest one, which was found only a **hundred** years ago, of how to make candles from **wax** and string: also, how to make glass, which is put in our windows to protect us from the **rain**. To find these things, the **scholars** must study the **earth** and learn from the rivers, from the sands, from the winds and the rocks. And if we went to the Home of the Scholars, we could learn from these also. We could ask **questions** of these, for they do not forbid questions.

LESSON 8
Exercise 1
1.

WHAT DO I KNOW ABOUT THIS TOPIC?	WHAT DO I WANT TO LEARN ABOUT THIS TOPIC?
The Cuban Revolution was led by Fidel Castro.	What caused Cubans to migrate to the United States?
The revolution affected the economy and international relations.	How did the United States respond to Cuban immigrants?
Many people attempted to flee Cuba.	

3. Part A: c
   Part B: b

4. In 1962, President John F. Kennedy expanded the Cuban Refugee Program through the "Migration and Refugee Assistance Act." This act provided financial and educational aid, as well as housing, healthcare and childcare for Cubans who were entering the country each week.

5.

WHAT HAVE I LEARNED ABOUT THE TOPIC?
• The Cuban Revolution led to many Cubans migrating to the United States. • I learned that President Dwight Eisenhower and President John F. Kennedy established programs to help Cuban migrants with education, health, finances and housing. • The Cuban Adjustment Act allowed Cuban refugees who lived in the United States for two years the opportunity to get permanent residency. • Approximately 1,500-2,000 Cubans arrived in the United States weekly.

Exercise 2

2. Part A

i. "Gloom" refers to a state of sadness or darkness.

ii. "Countenance" refers to one's facial expression.

Part B

*As I spoke, a dark **despair** spread over my listener's **expression**.*

Practice Exercise

1. a. Un-happy-ly
   b. In-corrigible
   c. In-dignation
   d. Occasion-ally

2. Part A: This passage is a description of the wealthy Mr. Stryver, who is ambitious and conniving. He has married a widow with three sons who he does not believe are well-mannered.
   Part B:
   - Mr. Stryver was rich: had married a florid widow with property and three boys, who had nothing particularly shining about them but the straight hair of their dumpling heads.
   - The polite rejection of the three lumps of bread-and-cheese had quite bloated Mr. Stryver with indignation, which he afterwards turned to account in the training of the young gentlemen...
   - Some of his King's Bench familiars, who were occasionally parties to the full-bodied wine and the lie, excused him for the latter by saying that he had told it so often, that he believed it himself...

3. a. This simile means that Mr. Stryver was ambitious and determined to succeed in the field of law.
   b. This simile means that Mr. Stryver used his friend to succeed and then left him behind.

4. Part A: Yes, Mrs. Stryver was rich when Mr. Stryver married her.
   Part B: The excerpt states that she already had property before she got married.

5. Part A: Yes, Mr. Stryver likes to drink wine.
   Part B: The line "he was also in the habit of declaiming to Mrs. Stryver, over his full-bodied wine..." shows that he enjoys drinking wine with high alcohol content.

LESSON 9
Exercise 1
- Van Helsing is resilient as this is the first time the narrator ever saw him break down.
- Van Helsing is also compassionate as he feels pity for the woman. He states, "What have we done, what has this poor thing done, that we are so sore beset?...This poor mother, all unknowing, and all for the best as she thinks, does such thing as lose her daughter body and soul..."

Exercise 2
1. Indirect: Freddy easily reached the highest cupboard while we needed to stand on chairs to reach it.
2. Direct: I did not understand the text.
3. Direct: Talia is determined and pushes her limits.

Exercise 3
Some students are quick and clever as they skip more than half of their lessons. This is evident in the line, "those who were nimble skipped over half with impunity." Other students were slower and had more difficulty in their lessons, as described in the line, "those who were tardy had a smart application now and then in the rear, to quicken their speed or help them over a tall word."

Exercise 4
The boys were heartless as they flung stones at the horses to make them gallop.
The men were unkind as they roughly handled Ginger while she was scared and did not understand what they wanted from her.

Practice Exercise
1. i. a
   ii. a
   iii. d
   iv. c

2. George cares deeply about his family. He is worried about his son's future and wishes that he and Eliza never met as they must now separate.

3. George means that a parent will be hurt each time the world is unkind to their child and takes advantage of their child's best qualities.

4. After this scene, the couple may run away to escape the injustice and cruelty of slavery and protect their young son.

5. President Lincoln was speaking about 87 years ago.

6. President Lincoln displays patriotism in this speech as he states that "we here highly resolve that these dead shall not have died in vain: that this nation shall have a new birth of freedom."

7. d

8. Mr. Phillips is unfair as he chooses to punish and humiliate Anne alone although a dozen students were disobedient.

9. Part A: b
   Part B: a

10. Anne is proud. This is shown when she rises haughtily from her seat after Mr. Phillips orders her to sit with the boys.

11. Anne might have decided to leave school after the scene due to Mr. Phillips' unjust punishment.

12.
   - Amy is artistic as she draws portraits of her family and sketches scenes from nature.
   - She is determined as she continues to practice her skills despite the obstacles she faces.
   - She is also innovative as she experiments with different art mediums and subjects.

13. a

14. Part A: a
    Part B: c

15. Part A: b
    Part B: b

LESSON 10
Exercise 1
Visual: tired, dusty, splintery
Auditory: the sound of the bats hitting the ball; creaky
Tactile: empty bellies, thirsty, parched throats

Exercise 2
1. A metaphor is being used in the lyrics.
2. The writer compares the beating of his heart to the music on a stereo. His heart beats for his loved one, and the metaphor implies that he will be there to comfort and support her like how music comforts others.

Exercise 3
The speaker, who is a child, is dancing with his intoxicated father. Since the father is intoxicated, he is unsteady and the speaker has to hold onto him tightly so he does not fall or get hurt. During this dance, the speaker's mother observes disapprovingly.

Practice Exercise

1.   This passage is about a crew's attempt to capture a whale.
2.   Part A: b

     Part B: a
3.   Part A: c

     Part B: b
4.   The passage reminds me of the times I saw whales on television and watched a documentary on the behavior of whales.
5.   This scene ends with Moby Dick killing Ahab while he tries to catch the whale. This is evident as the passage states that Ahab gets flung off the boat numerous times: "had it not been for the elevated part of the gunwale to which he then clung, Ahab would once more have been tossed into the sea."
6.   The theme of the poem is the fear of a rival.
7.   This poem reminds me of a classmate who would make fun of me and mockingly say my name.
8.   The poet has evoked the visual sense through the use of phrases such as "I see him on the cliff!" and "if he should look this way, and if/he's got his telescope!"
9.   The poet has evoked the auditory sense through the use of phrases such as "a little whisper at my ear" and "bellow out my name in tones."
10.   The song's theme is about having courage.
11.   The writer has evoked the visual sense through words such as "spineless" and "pale."

LESSON 11
Exercise 1
This passage is considered written in the first person because it contains first-person pronouns such as "I" and "our." This indicates that the narrator is giving a first-hand account of the events.

Exercise 2
This is considered a third-person narration because it only uses third-person pronouns such as "he," "his" and "their."

Practice Exercise

1.   The first-person point of view is used in the passage.
2.   This is evident as the excerpt begins with the first-person pronoun, "I."
3.   The passage is in the third-person point of view.
4.   This is evident as it only uses the third-person pronouns "he" and "him."
5.   The passage is in the first-person narration.
6.   The narrator uses the first-person pronoun, "I." Furthermore, he participates in the events, so the reader gets a first-hand account of what is taking place.
7.   The first-person point of view is used in the passage.
8.   This is evident as the first-person pronoun is used in the passage. Furthermore, the narrator is also a participant in the events, so the reader gets a first-hand account of his thoughts and feelings.

LESSON 12
Exercise 1
5. Agate had the lowest cost in 1893.
6. Pica cost the most in 1866.
7. Diamond had the highest cost between 1841 and 1866.
8. No, Lg. Primer did not have the highest cost in 1893.
9. Bourgeois cost the cheapest in 1893.
10. Nonpareil had the highest cost between 1806 and 1841.
11. Minion had the highest cost in 1811.
12. Nonpareil showed a decline in price.

Exercise 2
1. The same number of students were late on Tuesday and Thursday.
2. Thirty students were late on Monday.
3. Five more students were late on Friday as compared to Tuesday.
4. Many students were late on Monday because they were still in weekend mode and may have woken up late or moved more slowly when getting ready.

Exercise 3
2. The slowest time is 30 minutes and 26 seconds.
3. The letter "S" represents "Silver" since Vivian won the silver medal.
5. Most winners represented Kenya.
6. If I had won the gold medal, I would have felt grateful and proud of myself because I would have trained and sacrificed a lot to achieve it.

Practice Exercises
1. Tuna and sweetcorn sold the most.
2. Pizza with no topping sold the least.
3. Four no-topping pizzas were sold.
4. Nine cheese-only pizzas were sold.
5. The difference is fourteen.
6. The no-topping pizzas did not sell much because they would not have been flavorful like the pizzas with various toppings.
7. August was the warmest.
8. February was the coldest.
9. The biggest temperature change occurred between August and September.
10. The temperature in June was 56 degrees.
11. The weather would have been sunny and hot in August.
12. Part A: Yes, the overall cost decreases.
    Part B: In the second row, twelve ships and ninety guns were purchased, totaling £358,632. In the third row, the same number of ships were bought but with eighty guns. The total, which is £283,656, is lower than the total for the second row.
13. The Navy spent £496,895 when they bought 35 ships.
14. The Navy spent £424,240 when they bought 50 guns.
15. The Navy spent £170,000 when they did not buy any guns.

LESSON 13

1. I can infer that Madame Defarge is keeping watch over the customers and secretly tells her husband to pay special attention to them.
2. Madame Defarge's purpose is to keep watch.
3. Madame Defarge is watchful, secretive, strong and composed.
4. a. asserted
    b. things that are calculated or counted
    c. to be in charge of something
5. The coldness seemed to penetrate my skin, so I wrapped the fur and numerous bright shawls around my head and shoulders. After, I adjusted my large, gleaming earrings to ensure they were still in view. Feeling a chicken bone stuck in my teeth, I laid down my knitting and began to pick my teeth with a toothpick.
6. I can infer that Tom cares deeply about Becky Thatcher, so he worries a lot when she is ill. His worry results in him abandoning his hobbies. He keeps his feelings to himself and does not tell his aunt, perhaps because he is uncomfortable telling her. Thus, she becomes concerned about his unusual behavior and tries various remedies on him.
7. Part A: Tom lost interest in war, piracy, and playing with his bat and hoop.
    Part B: He lost interest because he was worried about Becky Thatcher who was ill.
8. Tom's aunt was fascinated with different remedies and enjoyed experimenting with them on people other than herself because she did not trust them.
9. I've felt like that when I was worried about not being able to save enough money. During this time, my brother became ill, and I became busy caring for him.
10. I can infer that the rabbit is a stuffed toy that can think and feel. The boy cares about the rabbit but still neglects him in some ways, and the adults do not see the rabbit's value.
11. During the spring, animals and people enjoy the outdoors and use the time to socialize and explore.
12. After this scene, the woman probably washed the velveteen rabbit before giving him back to the boy.
13. a. fell
    b. held
14. The character would like to be a real rabbit, and he appreciates the boy's attempts to treat him like one.
15. I can infer that the bride did not want to be married and thus ran away. The lady who attempted to enter the house may have spoken truthfully and the bride knew of her.
16. The bride's father, Mr. Aloysius Doran, the Duchess of Balmoral and Lord Backwater attended the ceremony.
    (Answer may also include Lord Eustace, Lady Clara St. Simon and Lady Alicia Whittington.)
17. a. extended
    b. banished
    c. servant
18. The writer means that the woman's disappearance was linked to criminal behavior. The police officers arrested the woman who tried to enter the house as they believed she had a reason to hurt the bride.
19. Part A: The sentence is in the third-person point of view.

Part B: I entered the house and sat with the others to have breakfast. However, I could not eat as my mind was preoccupied with the thought of being married. When my stomach began hurting, I complained to my father about it and then sought solace in my bedroom.

REFERENCES

1. The Secret Garden by Frances Hodgson Burnett (1910)
2. The Innocence of Father Brown by G. K. Chesterton (1911)
3. Dracula by Bram Stoker (1897)
4. None Other Gods by Robert Hugh Benson (1910)
5. The Legend of Sleepy Hollow by Washington Irving (1820)
6. Frankenstein: Or, The Modern Prometheus by Mary Wollstonecraft Shelley (1823)
7. ION by PLATO (No date)
8. A Tale Of Two Cities: A Story Of The French Revolution by Charles Dickens (1859)
9. The Jungle Book by Rudyard Kipling (1894)
10. Little Women by Louisa May Alcott (1869)
11. The Adventures of Tom Sawyer by Mark Twain (1876)
12. Uncle Tom's Cabin by Harriet Beecher Stowe (1852)
13. President Abraham Lincoln's 1863 Gettysburg Address
14. Anne of Green Gables by Lucy Maud Montgomery (1908)
15. The American Printer: A Manual of Typography by Thomas MacKellar (1885)
16. Common Sense by Thomas Paine (1776)
17. Goodbye, Mr. Chips by James Hilton (1938)
18. Great Expectations by Charles Dickens (1861)
19. The Hound of the Baskervilles by Sir Arthur Conan Doyle (1902)
20. Gulliver's Travels into Several Remote Nations of the World by Jonathan Swift (1926)
21. Pride and Prejudice by Jane Austen (1813)
22. The Adventures of Sherlock Holmes by Arthur Conan Doyle (1876)
23. The Wonderful Wizard of Oz by L. Frank Baum (1900)
24. Anthem by Ayn Rand (1937)
25. Moby-Dick Or, The Whale by Herman Melville (1851)
26. A Journal of the Plague Year by Daniel Defoe (1722)
27. Kidnapped by Robert Louis Stevenson (1886)

ARTICLES

- "Ethnolinguistic groups present in Afghanistan in 1992" (Sourced from Digital Public Library of America: https://dp.la/item/4b1aee91f958a068fd16141a83cf03ed?q=pie%20chart)
- "Exploration of the Americas" (Sourced from Digital Public Library of America: https://dp.la/primary-source-sets/exploration-of-the-americas)
- "Frank Lloyd Wright and Modern American Architecture" (Sourced from Digital Public Library of America: https://dp.la/primary-source-sets/frank-lloyd-wright-and-modern-american-architecture).
- "The Columbian Exchange" (Sourced from Digital Public Library of America: https://dp.la/primary-source-sets/the-columbian-exchange)
- "Powhatan People and the English at Jamestown" (Sourced from Digital Public Library of America: https://dp.la/primary-source-sets/powhatan-people-and-the-english-at-jamestown)
- "To Kill a Mockingbird by Harper Lee" (Sourced from Digital Public Library of America: https://dp.la/primary-source-sets/to-kill-a-mockingbird-by-harper-lee)

- "The Woman Warrior by Maxine Hong Kingston" (Sourced from Digital Public Library of America: https://dp.la/primary-source-sets/the-woman-warrior-by-maxine-hong-kingston)
- Barack Obama's Speech on the 50th Anniversary of the Selma Marches
- "Cuban Immigration After the Revolution, 1959-1973" (Sourced from Digital Public Library of America: https://dp.la/primary-source-sets/cuban-immigration-after-the-revolution-1959-1973)
- "California Gold Rush' (Sourced from Digital Public Library of America: https://dp.la/primary-source-sets/california-gold-rush)
- "The American Whaling Industry" (Sourced from Digital Public Library of America: https://dp.la/primary-source-sets/the-american-whaling-industry)
- Commodore Perry's Expedition to Japan (Sourced from Digital Public Library of America: https://dp.la/primary-source-sets/commodore-perry-s-expedition-to-japan)
- "The Awakening by Kate Chopin" (Sourced from Digital Public Library of America: https://dp.la/primary-source-sets/the-awakening-by-kate-chopin)
- "Theodore Dreiser's Sister Carrie and the Urbanization of Chicago" (Sourced from Digital Public Library of America: https://dp.la/primary-source-sets/theodore-dreiser-s-sister-carrie-and-the-urbanization-of-chicago)
- "Pop Art in the US" (Sourced from Digital Public Library of America: https://dp.la/primary-source-sets/pop-art-in-the-us)
- Lyndon Johnson's Great Society (Sourced from Digital Public Library of America https://dp.la/primary-source-sets/lyndon-johnson-s-great-society)

Poems

- "Phantasmagoria and Other Poems: A Sea Dirge" by Lewis Carroll (1911)
- "Ozymandias" by Percy Bysshe Shelley (1818)
- "The Rime of the Ancient Mariner" by Samuel Taylor Coleridge (1834)
- "The Base Stealer" by Robert Francis (1976)
- "Phantasmagoria and Other Poems: Size and Tears" by Lewis Carroll (1911)
- "Phantasmagoria and Other Poems: Canto VI - Dyscomfyture" by Lewis Carroll (1911)
- "The Bells" by Edgar Allan Poe (1849)
- "Poems, Series 1" by Emily Dickinson
- "My November Guest" by Robert Frost (1915)
- "Fish" by Elizabeth Bishop (1911)
- "Summer Night" by Alfred Tennyson (unknown)
- "My Papa's Waltz" by Theodore Rothke (1942)

Other

A climate graph for the District of Columbia (Sourced from: https://www.usclimatedata.com/)

ABOUT COACHING FOR BETTER LEARNING, LLC

CBL helps develop systems that increase performance and save time, resources and energy.

If you identify typos and errors in the text, p lease let us know at coachingforbetterlearning@gmail.com. We promise to fix them and send you a free copy of the updated textbook to thank you.

Made in United States
Orlando, FL
30 July 2024

49739498R00079